STILL BORED IN A CULTURE OF ENTERTAINMENT

REDISCOVERING PASSION AND WONDER

RICHARD WINTER

InterVarsity Press
Downers Grove, Illinois

InterVarsity Press
P.O. Box 1400, Downers Grove, IL 60515-1426
World Wide Web: www.ivpress.com
E-mail: mail@ivpress.com

InterVarsity Press® is the book-publishing division of InterVarsity Christian Fellowship/USA®, a student
movement active on campus at hundreds of universities, colleges and schools of nursing in the United States of
America, and a member movement of the International Fellowship of Evangelical Students. For information
about local and regional activities, write Public Relations Dept., InterVarsity Christian Fellowship/USA, 6400
Schroeder Rd., P.O. Box 7895, Madison, WI 53707-7895, or visit the IVCF website at <www.ivcf.org>.

Cover photograph: Dandy Zipper/Getty Images

ISBN 0-8308-2308-5

Printed in the United States of America ∞

Library of Congress Cataloging-in-Publication Data

Winter, Richard, 1945-
  Still bored in a culture of entertainment: rediscovering passion &
wonder/Richard Winter.
      p. cm.
  Includes bibliographical references.
  ISBN 0-8308-2308-5 (pbk.: alk. paper)
  1. Boredom—Religious aspects—Christianity. 2. Christian life. I.
Title.
  BV4599.5.B67 W56 2002
  241'.3—dc21
                                                                  2002007428

P	18	17	16	15	14	13	12	11	10	9	8	7	6	5	4	3	2	1
Y	16	15	14	13	12	11	10	09	08	07	06	05	04	03	02

CONTENTS

ACKNOWLEDGMENTS

My thanks to many special people: Kim Goff for her patience during the many hours she spent checking a very large number of rather obscure references and quotes; Jen Morley for her help with the final details of the work; Covenant Theological Seminary for the encouragement and time to work on this project; Gardner West for his help with chapter summaries; David Calhoun for his helpful comments on medieval boredom in chapter eight: Patricia Spacks for the inspiration of her book on boredom; Francis Schaeffer and all my friends and colleagues at L'Abri who have encouraged and inspired me, for many years, to be a student and critic of culture; and to Wade Bradshaw who startled me one day, after helping me with my original article on boredom, when he said "There's a book in this!"

Thanks to my children: to Johanna and John for their helpful suggestions and editing of the early drafts; to Matthew, Anna and Rebecca for their long-distance encouragement across the Atlantic Ocean; and to Triona, the last of my children still at home, for her uncomplaining spirit in the face of my writing "absences."

Last but far from least, my thanks to my dear companion and wife, Jane, for her helpful comments on the manuscript and her patience, encouragement and hard work while I spent many hours researching and writing when I could have been pursuing a more lucrative occupation!

INTRODUCTION

NOBODY WAS BORED ON SEPTEMBER 11, 2001. On that day and for several weeks afterward we were all transfixed by the terrible unfolding drama at the Twin Towers and the Pentagon. The casts of Broadway shows wondered whether they should and could continue their performances. It felt wrong to go to a movie or a concert. For the first week after the attacks, many events were canceled or postponed. People stayed at home, afraid to take risks in the threatening world outside, and remained glued to the television news. The culture of entertainment seemed to shrivel and become redundant overnight. Only the advertisements for medication to relieve anxiety seemed relevant. David Letterman and Jay Leno were more serious than they had ever been. It was hard to laugh at much except as a brief temporary relief from the hundreds of tragic stories that filled the news. Two New York papers temporarily suspended their satirical comic strips. One month after the event, Darren Star, creator of *Sex and the City* and *Beverly Hills 90210*, said in an interview with the *New York Times:*

> *Sex and the City* always took as its core material this great frisson of silliness and fashion and an enormous amount of money and superficiality. We had fun with it, we celebrated it, we did a lot of things with it. And now there is a shifting mood. . . . The first non-news I watched after all this happened was

the season premiere of *Friends*. Until then, I'd been thinking, Who cares about make-believe TV? But then *Friends* was funny, and it made me laugh—partly because I knew nothing terrible was going to happen to these people.[1]

Certainly at first, people were more open to serious discussion about ultimate issues like good and evil, the meaning of life and the importance of spending time with family. Our cultural heroes changed within a few hours from Hollywood stars and sports legends to courageous firefighters and police officers.

Now, months later, we are used to the new realities and the entertainment industry has regained its stride. Even the endless articles and programs on Islam and the war in Afghanistan only held our attention for a time and soon became boring in their repetition. For a while I wondered whether this book would be irrelevant after September 11, but for most people little about the daily routines of life has really changed; and until the next moment of high drama in real life, many of us will still find our daily excitement on *ER*, *Survivor* or *Temptation Island*. Last night we went to a movie at yet another new megaplex cinema with multiple screens. It was packed!

There is a certain irony about the fact that this book began a few years ago when I was asked to do a lecture on boredom in Orlando, Florida, just a stone's throw from the mecca of entertainment, Disney World. After questioning whether anything interesting could be said about boredom, I began some research and found myself so intrigued that the lecture grew into an article, and it was not long before the article had become an embryonic book. As I began my research my curiosity was aroused when I discovered Patricia Spacks's fascinating and masterly overview of the theme of boredom in English literature titled *Boredom: The Literary History of a State of Mind*. Spacks sketches four hypotheses about the increased importance of boredom in the last two hundred years: the development of leisure, the decline of Christianity, the increased concern for individual rights and the increasing interest in inner experience. In her final paragraph Spacks writes:

> The history of boredom in its cultural constructions matters partly because boredom itself now appears to matter so much. If boredom can provide plausible justification for acts of violence or self-destruction, if the desire to forestall it sells fountain pens and trips around the world, if fiction writers assume

it as the substratum of experience and journalists draw on it as a readily comprehensible realm of reference—if all of the above are true, it would seem that boredom has assumed broad explanatory power in a society widely felt to be baffling.[2]

My book is an attempt to understand some of the complexities of this often-confusing world in which we live.

To try to do justice to a subject which "matters" that much, I have explored it from many angles—sociological, psychological, historical, theological and practical—in a search for the causes of boredom and the ways we might counteract it. This search will take us to the heart of the problem and the potential of the human condition in the twenty-first century.

1

THREE YAWNS FOR BOREDOM!

WE HAD BEEN SIX HOURS IN THE AIR and there were four hours left to go! I had eaten, dozed, watched a movie, finished my book and read a newspaper, and now I was thoroughly bored. My thoughts drifted back to the long hours I spent in the back seat of the car as a small boy, driving to a summer vacation with my brother and two sisters. Every half hour one of us would ask, "Are we there yet, Mommy?" or "How much farther, Daddy?"

Recently I drove twenty hours alone and nonstop from Boston to St. Louis. Fortunately I had something to keep my ears and brain active—a series of fascinating interviews and a book on tape, which were a great help in keeping me going. I found myself alternating between the interviews, the book and radio station surfing to keep me from boredom. My eyes and other senses enjoyed the rolling farmland of southern New York state, and thankfully there was not much traffic. A few strange quirks of my behavior amused me and made me realize how much *all* my senses craved stimulation. I was taking food home from a vacation house, and just behind my seat was a large packet of Honey Nut Cheerios. I probably ate at least two thirds of that packet in those twenty hours, little by little, at times just five or six Cheerios every few minutes. I also had some sandwiches that helped relieve the monotony. From time to time I would stretch and shake and even slap myself quite hard.

I shouted, daydreamed, sang, talked to myself, prayed and laughed. Three times I got dangerously sleepy and the yawn count began to creep up so I stopped for a nap. I was fascinated by how I dealt with boredom and how each of my senses cried out for help! The first and last hours were the worst.

Now let your imagination wander. Imagine you have an evening free: nothing to do, no responsibilities for other people. I wonder what your first thought is. A movie? A video or two? Imagine what it would be like to have no television, no computer, no videos and no movies! We find it hard to conceive of such an existence; in fact, some would find it frightening. What would we do with ourselves? How would we survive the famine of entertainment? I suppose a major power failure could give us a taste of what it would be like. What did previous generations do with themselves?

To test the level of your dependence on electronic entertainment, try, for twenty-four hours—or if you are brave, for several days, even a week—to not listen to radio, tapes or CDs; to not watch television or videos; and to not go to movies. How will you manage to drive to work each day without the radio? Someone who tried this test found that her hand kept going to the radio switch. She dealt with this temptation by singing aloud every song she could remember. What would you do with yourself without television?

Even without a power failure or an entertainment fast, and even with all the distractions, diversions and amusements of our day, many people are still bored. Here in St. Louis I was aware of the huge interest in baseball as the Cardinals progressed toward the World Series. At the same time there was a football frenzy with tens of thousands of fans cheering the Rams. Hundreds of concerts throughout the city, multiple movies available at cinemas and videos, dozens of channels on television to watch at home—how could anyone be bored? Yet a recent annual study of the opinions of consumers revealed a paradoxical "boredom boom": "we are bored despite living in remarkable times." This survey found that in 1999, 71 percent of approximately 2,500 respondents surveyed desired more novelty as a part of their lives, an increase of 4 percent from 1998. "Just as a drug user develops a tolerance and needs larger doses to achieve the same effect, so too have we developed a tolerance to amazing events."[1]

This trend was highlighted some years ago in a *Reader's Digest* article titled "How to Cope with Boredom":

> Despite its extraordinary variety of diversions and resources, its frenzy for spectacles and its feverish pursuit of entertainment, America is bored. The abundance of efforts made in the United States to counter boredom have defeated themselves, and boredom has become the disease of our time.[2]

Some people may be acutely aware of being bored, though most would probably see the theme of this article as an extreme exaggeration. Yet others are also raising the alarm. In Britain a recent article in a major national newspaper titled "You're Bored, Damned Bored" reported the archbishop of Wales saying:

> We are a deeply, dangerously bored society. And we're reluctant to look for the root of that. Why do we want to escape from the glories and difficulties of everyday life? Why do we want to escape into gambling or drugs or any other kind of fantasy?
>
> Why have we created a culture which seems more in love with fantasy than reality? Whether that's gambling or drugs or, for that matter, the national lottery, we should be asking, "What's happened to us? Why are we so bored?"[3]

When I was first invited to speak on the topic of boredom, I wondered why anyone would be interested in it. "We would like you to speak on boredom," the inviting committee said, "because there are plenty of people around here who seem bored with life." I imagine that the people who invited me to speak might have recognized something that is very familiar in Professor Reinhard Kuhn's portrait of the typical suburbanite:

> She is tired of the magazine that she is reading or the television show that she is watching and mixes another cocktail for herself. Or perhaps she telephones an equally bored friend and they talk for hours about nothing, or perhaps she drifts into an affair that means as little to her as the television show or the magazine article.[4]

We all know only too well the teenager who has "nothing to do." There is nothing on television that catches his interest, his friends are all busy, and he expects others to come up with something for him to do as he exclaims repeatedly, "I'm bored!"

In one poll, it was found that "the most common response to boredom [was] 'to switch TV channels.' " Of those people surveyed, 44 percent said they eat when they are bored, and 27 percent said they go for a drive.[5]

Why is it that in an age when we have more entertainment available to us than ever before, there seems to be an epidemic of boredom? Does it seem extreme to talk about boredom in this way? Whenever I have lectured on this subject, people have been only vaguely interested in the beginning of the lecture. But as they begin to think about it, they realize how common boredom is in their own lives or in the lives of their children or their friends. Even if they have never used the word *boring* to describe the dreary times of life, it is almost as if I put their previously unarticulated feelings into words. In the question-and-answer time, there is a liveliness and engagement with the topic that was certainly not felt at the beginning of the presentation. No one is bored with the topic! The material resonates strangely and powerfully with their souls.

BORING OR EXCITING?

Think of the synonyms for *boring*. Consider them slowly. Let them sink into your mind. Feel them. *Apathetic, drab, dull, colorless, humdrum, insipid, interminable, irksome, lifeless, lethargic, monotonous, mundane, repetitious, routine, stale, stodgy, tedious, tiresome, uninteresting, vapid, wearisome. Bor-ing,* as teenagers would say with a tone of disgust. We speak of being "bored to death," "out of my mind with boredom," "bored to tears" and "bored beyond belief." It is obviously a distressing, uncomfortable state of mind, from which we desire to escape: an experience of there being nothing that we desire to do. Even more distressing is that we have an active desire not to do the things that are available.

Now think of the opposite. Again, let yourself feel these words: *interesting, absorbing, amusing, attractive, captivating, charismatic, compelling, delightful, engaging, engrossing, enthralling, entrancing, exotic, fascinating, gripping, riveting, stimulating—exciting.*[6] Notice how many times you hear *exciting* in the coming week. How often have you heard in the last week: *"I'm so excited!"* There is little desire to escape this experience.

"To bore" means to weary "by being dull, uninteresting, or monotonous."[7] It has a mildly aggressive connotation, as if one were literally, slowly and steadily boring (i.e., piercing into something or someone). I felt this myself once when I asked one of my students why she never participated in class discussions. She responded quickly and slightly sarcastically, "To be honest, I am bored. I have covered a lot of this material in previous classes." This sharp needle of a comment punctured the bubble of my ego, and I smarted for a few hours, wondering whether my class, which I had redesigned specifically to make it more interesting, was really that boring!

Ambrose Bierce catches something of another sense of being attacked, or drilled into, when he defines the noun *bore* as "a person who talks when you wish him to listen!"[8] This situation prompts irritation and a desire to respond in kind—a bore for a bore! When someone, in an open discussion, talks on and on, full of his own opinions and insensitive to the opinions of others, I almost invariably feel profoundly bored and irritated—I feel like telling him to "shut up," and I have a strong desire to escape. In one study, researchers asked individuals what they found boring in others, and some of the characteristics described were passivity, tediousness, seriousness, self-preoccupation and banality.[9]

Now as I have hinted already, one of the strange things about this state of mind is that people, until they are forced to think about it, may not have identified their feeling as boredom. They may recognize that they are frustrated, depressed or irritable, but they probably have not recognized that they are bored. In most situations we still have a negative response to a complaint of boredom: the complaint might be seen as a fault, and therefore it may not be wise to admit it openly. Our lack of awareness of our boredom may also be, as sociologist Orrin Klapp says, because "placebo institutions such as entertainment, gambling, sports, drugs, and media may be palliating or masking boredom so that people do not realize their own hidden hungers."[10] These institutions act as cultural tranquilizers or sedatives, taking away our uncomfortable awareness of the monotony and tedium of reality.

A HISTORY LESSON

History lessons, in a small private school in England, were for me the most boring classes of all, with endless recitation of the kings and queens of the realm and their dates. Now that I have been tracing my family tree back to 1600, I have been fascinated by what was going on in earlier centuries. But in the classroom, at the end of a long day, what relevance did it have to a ten-year-old boy?

In order to understand anything really well, we have to look back at its origin and development. To understand who you are as a person, it is very helpful to look at your family roots; what you were like as a child, teenager and young adult; and the influences that shaped you. So, at risk of losing your attention and producing a few yawns, I will take you on our first of several brief journeys into the past to understand how society's concept of boredom was shaped.

No one knows the exact origin of the word *boredom*, but Professor Patricia Spacks says that the word was not used in the English language until after 1750.

> The first occurrence cited comes from a private letter of 1768, Earl Carlisle announcing his pity for "Newmarket friends, who are to be bored by those Frenchmen." Bore, meaning "a thing which bores," comes along in 1778; the bore as tiresome person is assigned to 1812; . . . the first citation of the noun boredom belongs to 1864.[11]

Spacks documents an increasing preoccupation with boredom in the literature and culture from that time. She sees boredom as "a metaphor for the postmodern condition."[12] It seems to have entered the English language from the French thinkers of the seventeenth century who wrote about "ennui." In 1670 Blaise Pascal referred to "man's condition as that of inconstancy, boredom [ennui], and anxiety"[13] and wrote "no matter how happy a man may be, if he lacks distraction and has no absorbing passion or pastime to keep boredom away, he will soon get depressed and unhappy."[14] Jacques Bossuet wrote of "this incurable ennui, which forms the very basis of life."[15] Charles Baudelaire, a "prophet of boredom," wrote about it frequently and vividly, and elevated it above every other vice. About Baudelaire's "Les Fleurs du Mal" (the flowers of sickness), Seán Healy writes, "Boredom seems suddenly to emerge with all its modern characteristics: intense, desperate, agonized, undirected irritation alternating with a sullen,

morose, lowering lethargy and an utterly exasperated violence."[16] Boredom
is often accompanied by feelings of lethargy, irritation and anger.

A *Dictionarie of the French and English Tongues,* published in the early
seventeenth century, translates *ennui* as "annoy; vexation; trouble; disqui-
et; sorrow; grief; anguish; wearisomeness; tediousness; irksomenesse . . . a
discontentment."[17] The French word has a stronger flavor of sadness than
the English word does. Shakespeare uses the word *weary* to describe the experience of boredom: "I stay too long by thee, I weary thee," says Henry
IV.[18] Spacks shows how Samuel Johnson and James Boswell, reflecting on
the tedium of life in their own times (the eighteenth century), use words
like *vacuity* and *satiety.*[19] Logan Pearsall Smith, an eminent expert in the origin of words, notes that "when anything becomes important to us it finds
its name."[20] Perhaps the emergence of the word *boredom* into the English
language is the first sign or symptom of a disease that would spread like a
plague over the next three hundred years. Kuhn, in his study of ennui in
literature, says that by the twentieth century, it is "not one theme among
others; it is the dominant theme . . . a modern plague."[21] Klapp also demonstrates the rising incidence of ennui, despair and apathy in literature, art,
theater and cinema. He claims that

> a strange cloud hangs over modern life. At first it was not noticed; now it is
> thicker than ever. It embarrasses claims that the quality of life is getting bet-
> ter. It reduces commitment to work. It is thickest in cities where there are
> the most varieties, pleasure, and opportunities. Like smog, it spreads to all
> sorts of places it is not supposed to be. The most common name for this cloud
> is boredom.[22]

Once we have looked at the many causes of boredom, we will be in a better position to answer the question of what it was about that time in history
and culture that gave rise to this "disease." We will also have a better understanding of the strange phenomenon of the apparent increase of boredom in the last three hundred years. There is plenty of evidence that
boredom has always existed, but perhaps there are times and circumstances
that exacerbate this problem.

2

BASICS OF BOREDOM

Understimulation, Repetition and Disconnection

WHEN PEOPLE ARE ASKED ABOUT experiences of boredom, they usually recall times of monotony and understimulation: a long lecture on an uninteresting subject delivered in a monotone voice; a three-hour committee
meeting; several weeks in hospital; or even, to use an extreme example, a
movie like Andy Warhol's extraordinary *Sleep*, where for eight long hours
the audience watches a person sleeping.

Extremes of sensory deprivation or understimulation have been demonstrated to produce compensatory activity in the brain. Sensory deprivation
was achieved, for example, when volunteers were put in a sound-insulated
room to lie still on a bed or in a tank of warm water, with their ears and eyes
covered, for many hours. In this state the volunteers began to experience
impaired thinking, irritability, restlessness, mood swings and hallucinations.
The latter were most commonly visual, but volunteers also heard voices and
music and felt things touching their skin. In another case, patients who
have major eye operations after which their eyes have to be covered for several days may begin to hallucinate and experience "black-patch psychosis."
Truck drivers who have spent many hours at the wheel on long, straight
roads may stop to pick up a nonexistent hitchhiker or may see "giant red
spiders on the windshield or non-existent animals running across the

road."[1] The drivers' brains, seeking some relief from the monotony, create the images in their minds.

Prisoners who survive years in solitary confinement have usually found some way to transform their incredibly bleak conditions into a controllable experience. Psychologist Mihaly Csikszentmihalyi comments on how they do this:

> Eve Zeisel, the ceramic designer who was imprisoned in Moscow's Lubyanka prison for over a year by Stalin's police, kept her sanity by figuring out how she would make a bra out of materials at hand, playing chess against herself in her head, holding imaginary conversations in French, doing gymnastics and memorizing poems she composed. Alexander Solzhenitsyn describes how one of his fellow prisoners in the Lefortovo jail mapped the world on the floor of the cell and then imagined himself traveling across Asia and Europe to America, covering a few kilometers each day. The same "game" was independently discovered by many prisoners; for instance Albert Speer, Hitler's favorite architect, sustained himself in Spandau prison for months by pretending he was taking a walking trip from Berlin to Jerusalem, in which his imagination provided all the events and sights along the way.[2]

Csikszentmihalyi tells the story of an American pilot who was shot down over North Vietnam and kept in a jungle prison camp for several years. He kept his sanity by playing an imaginary eighteen-hole golf course each day. This mental discipline helped to relieve boredom, and on his release he apparently played an extraordinary golf game, even though he was physically very weak.[3]

We are not made for monotony. Even rats in a maze will try to escape monotony by taking different routes to the food. Working for long hours at a repetitive task often produces dissatisfaction and inefficiency. Because of the monotony of their task, radar operators on antisubmarine patrol during World War II sometimes failed to detect U-boats; isolated operators had to stare at the screen for hours without a break. Experiments that required "subjects to watch a pointer moving around a graduated dial and to press a button whenever the pointer made a double jump" found that the "subjects' efficiency declined in the surprisingly short time of half an hour."[4] Airport-security checkers experience the same problem when watching baggage x-rays for hours on end. A director of the Aviation Institute at George Washington University said, "I was once able to do baggage screening for a week, and after about an hour, you could have driven a truck by me and I wouldn't have noticed."

A more common example comes from one of Peter Conrad's students who wrote about a recent experience of boredom:

> One Friday night. There I was, I had my license, a car to drive, friends I could hang out with, yet there I was—bored. There was nothing peaking my interest on TV—I didn't feel like staying in either. . . . [I] simply had no interest in doing anything, but didn't want to sit there and do nothing.[5]

Students in one study identified the most frequent causes of boredom as "classes and a lack of things to do, followed by a lack of challenge, monotony, loneliness, and having to wait."[6]

REPETITION'S BAD RAP

The boredom of certain jobs has been well documented. In the mid 1970s, Robert Kaplan found that out of twenty-three occupations, the top three most boring jobs were working on assembly lines, tending machines and running forklift trucks. Employees in these occupations had higher complaint rates for psychosomatic problems and depression than those in other occupations.[7]

Some fascinating research done by the British Industrial Fatigue Research Board in the 1920s throws light on the particular conditions that promote boredom. One research team found that semiautomated work produced more boredom than automated or nonautomated work: automated work allows time and space for social interaction with other workers; nonautomated work demands more concentration on the task in hand. Researchers also found that boredom was less likely if the worker was paid by the piece of work done, rather than for the time worked. They also found that there was less boredom when the workers worked in "compact social groups rather than as isolated units."[8] Other studies have shown the importance of interpersonal relationships in averting monotonous tasks. Sociologist J. M. Barbalet suggests that boredom is relieved by "fantasy," "play," "social interaction" and even "conflict."[9]

Higher up on the career ladder, writes Orrin Klapp:

> things are not all that much better. Even among young executives at middle
> management levels, a "creeping death" was reported. An editor of a trade jour-
> nal commented, "Boredom has crept from the assembly line all the way up to
> the executive suite." Firms launched antiboredom campaigns, hiring experts
> and trying job enrichment, job rotation, group assembly, and other ways, but
> many confessed a losing battle: that there was no ultimate escape from the te-
> dium of the machine—especially the human machine called bureaucracy.[10]

More recently it has been shown that many of the stresses associated
with working with computers are similar to the stresses associated with the
automated jobs of past decades. High workload, high work pressure, monotonous tasks and fear of job security have been joined by the stress of computer slowdowns or breakdowns and electronic performance monitoring.[11]

REPETITION REDEEMED

Connotations of the word *repetition* are almost always negative. As we have
seen, many jobs and tasks are tedious because they are essentially repetitive
and monotonous. But not all repetition is difficult and bad. Athletes who
compete in long-distance running or swimming events put up with an enormous amount of repetition. Musicians practice scales and exercises for long
hours every day in their desire to improve their ability and performance.
Dancers have to practice the same routines over and over again until the
steps become ingrained in their nervous systems and we experience the performance as a flow of spontaneous movement. There are many skills that
have to be learned by habitual repetition until they become good habits
that allow the freedom to be increasingly more creative.[12] Most people tolerate repetition when it clearly serves a greater goal. The ability to delay
gratification is part of one's emotional maturity. Understanding why repetition is necessary helps to make it less uncomfortable and even allows it to
be enjoyable. Behind most great medical breakthroughs lie long hours of tedious laboratory research. One rarely hears of these lab workers complaining of boredom. When repetition has a meaning and a purpose it is not
usually experienced as boring.

Some repetition is experienced as extremely enjoyable. My retriever will catch and bring back a Frisbee until he drops from exhaustion. Young children love to play games and hear stories in exactly the same way again and again. They seem to delight in knowing, but pretending not to know, what is going to happen next. My two-year-old grandson wants the same story read to him every day.

Perhaps there is security in repetition and in some of the rituals of each day. There is something deeply satisfying about familiar places and patterns. Children are often quite disturbed by a change of routine at bedtime. For years we have returned to a house on the coast of Maine for our summer vacation. There we have stored memories of laughter, games, good food, birds, seals, sailing, tennis, swimming, explorations and great natural beauty. We want to repeat those experiences as often as possible and share them with others.

In a powerful and mysterious way, beauty calls for repetition. We want to "capture" a beautiful person, a piece of music, a painting or a scene and repeat the encounter with beauty again and again. There is something sacred, life-giving and very profound that bears endless repetition. In the opening paragraphs of *On Beauty and Being Just,* Elaine Scarry reflects on the boyhood experiences of Leonardo da Vinci when he was apprenticed to the famous artist Andrea del Verrocchio:

> Beauty brings copies of itself into being. It makes us draw it, take photographs of it, or describe it to other people. Sometimes it gives rise to exact replication and other times to resemblances and still other times to things whose connection to the original site of inspiration is unrecognizable. A beautiful face drawn by Verrocchio suddenly glides into the perceptual field of a young boy named Leonardo. The boy copies the face, then copies the face again. Then again and again and again. He does the same thing when a beautiful living plant—a violet, a wild rose—glides into his field of vision, or a living face: he makes a first copy, a second copy, a third, a fourth, a fifth. He draws it over and over.[13]

When we reflect on the built-in rhythm and repetition of the seasons of nature and biological life, we see a wonderful diversity in the Creator's design that helps us value both routine and variety. Perhaps our hunger for novelty and stimulation has stunted our ability to see patterns and routines in the world with the innocence and wonder that we had as children.

Like many things in life, repetition is a mixed blessing—sometimes reassuring and good, sometimes tedious and boring.

DISCONNECTION

A sense of disconnection is another factor contributing to boredom. If I have no interest in golf or classical music, I will probably feel bored watching such a game or attending such a concert. I will likely be bored when I go to a lecture on a topic that has no relation to my life or experience. Even given a topic of some interest, if the lecturer drones on in a monotone voice, repeating himself or herself and barely engaging the audience, then I will probably disconnect and fall asleep if I cannot leave! If the subject is too complex for me to understand—or not complex enough to challenge me— a cloud of boredom may envelop me.

Peter Conrad found that

> students frequently blame teachers for "boring" classes. The one overwhelming characteristic they associate with boredom is the delivery of a lecture in a monotone voice. The lack of action makes it difficult for students to engage: "The professor never moved from his seat, spoke in a monotone voice, and seemed unaware (or uncaring) of this student's presence." . . . Perhaps this is where disconnection and understimulation meet to create a particularly powerful sense of boredom. The lack of action is also reflected in students attributing boredom due to an absence of interaction or participation in classes.[14]

Teachers have a difficult task today for they must compete with the sound bite and a culture of entertainment.

In a 1993 study, workers were asked when they were bored at work, and they said that it was when they had very little or nothing to do or when they were given simple, unchallenging tasks or overly difficult tasks.[15] Ideally we should find a job where we are neither overstimulated by too much information or challenge, nor understimulated by too much monotony and lack of challenge. An overload of challenge may induce stress from worry and fear, whereas too little challenge may induce stress from boredom and lack of interest.

BOREDOM AND THE LIFE CYCLE

There seem to be two peaks of boredom in the human life cycle—adolescence and old age. High school is the place many people associate with the greatest boredom. With the kind help of a teacher in a large public school in St. Louis, I did an informal survey of some students and found that the amount of boredom reported increased dramatically in students ages fifteen to sixteen years old. None said that they were never bored. A quarter said that they were occasionally bored, a third said they were sometimes bored, and another quarter said they were often bored. The students most often gave "waiting in line" or "being alone at home" as the reasons for short-term boredom. Approximately one-third of them said that there had been times when their boredom lasted more than four weeks. Girls seem to find being at home alone much more boring than do boys. The most popular activities for relieving boredom were talking to friends on the phone (cited by twice as many girls than boys), watching television (cited by twice as many girls than boys), playing music, singing or dancing, hanging out with friends or family and exercising (cited by more boys than girls).

A study of adolescent boredom in the *Journal of Leisure Research* found that teenagers who are engaged in an activity they have freely chosen are less likely to be bored than are those teenagers who have nothing else to do or who feel that they have to participate in an activity even though they are not inclined to do so.[16] When adolescents felt more in control of their own lives and choices, they experienced less boredom than when they were heavily influenced by parents or teachers.

For most of us who survive adolescence and early adulthood, the next big step is marriage. Sadly, some married couples do not understand how to keep a marriage alive, and they allow it to drift into a boring coexistence. Honore Daumier's eighteenth-century lithograph *Six Mois de Mariage* portrays a young couple, halfway through their first year of marriage, sitting together in their living room, yawning.

Many of the celebrity heroes of the contemporary music and movie industry are divorced within a few months or years of marriage. People with long lasting relationships learn to work through the inevitable times of conflict and boredom that occur in any marriage. They know that the feelings

of romantic excitement come and go, but where there is mutual commitment and a desire to really know and understand the other person there can
be deep companionship and lasting interest.

In the later stages of old age there comes a time for many people when
they are limited by loss of eyesight, hearing or mobility and are therefore re-
stricted in their ability to find things to do to relieve boredom. They may be
living alone or at a distance from their families, cut off from the stimulation
of relationships and other social interaction. They may find themselves in
nursing homes or hospitals. If their sense of identity and value is rooted in
their social or financial status, in their work or in their physical fitness or
golf handicap, then old age may well be full of frustration, boredom and a
sense of the meaninglessness of life. Those who have had lots of interests
earlier in life usually cope with the limitations of old age best of all.

As I write, my father has been in the hospital for three weeks now and
may have to stay awhile longer. Thankfully, he enjoys books and can still
read and watch television. But he is surrounded by elderly people who seem
utterly bored with life and who have little motivation left to find something
to do. They sleep their days away, half conscious, in front of the television.
Thankfully there are some good nursing homes that provide a variety of activities and a social life that help to combat isolation and boredom.

FOR RICHER OR POORER

In the world of nineteenth-century literature, authors often describe boredom among people who were rich, aristocratic and had everything they
needed—except enough entertainment. In *The Mill on the Floss*, George
Eliot gives a glimpse of such a lifestyle: "Good society has its claret and its
velvet carpets, its dinner-engagements six weeks deep, its opera and its faery
ball-rooms, [and] rides off its ennui on thoroughbred horses."[17] We see the
same situation today in the lifestyles of the rich and famous.

For those who own virtually nothing and wait out their days under the
bridges and on the streets of our cities, the experience of boredom is very
different. Alcoholic stupor, sleep, a chat with friends on a park bench or a
night in a shelter may be the only relief. Samuel Beckett's two tramps in
Waiting for Godot wile away the hours talking about nothing—"bored to

death"—waiting for the Big Answer that never comes.[18] Not only do the tramps illustrate the plight of such an existence but they also dramatically expose Beckett's profound pessimism as to whether any answers to the big questions of life exist.

Jerome Neu compares, rather condescendingly, the plight of the unintelligent and very poor with the plight of the intelligent and rich: "the uncultivated and the sophisticated are both bored, one because he notices and understands too little, the other because he notices and understands too much."[19]

In this chapter we have examined how understimulation, repetition and a sense of disconnection all contribute to boredom. It is helpful to delineate two main types of boredom because the causes and remedies may be very different, so I will do just that in the next chapter.

3

TWO TYPES OF BOREDOM

The Long and the Short of It

AS WE LOOK AT SOME OF THE REASONS for boredom, two common varieties are clearly evident. There is, first, the temporary boredom provoked by a repetitive job. A student told me that her most boring experience was "photocopying medical files eight hours a day, for two weeks, in a hospital basement." Boredom might be provoked by sitting through a long meeting, talking to someone at a party who speaks only about him- or herself, or enduring a long plane flight, an unchallenging job, a season of unemployment, a tedious sermon by a dull preacher, or a long lecture (or book) on boredom! Thankfully, there is usually a remedy for this type of boredom—find another job, go to sleep, walk out of a meeting or find some temporary distraction. I enjoy doodling to wile away the time during long lectures, sermons or committee meetings.

Second, there is longer-term and more permanent boredom in which there is nothing to do that one likes. *Webster's Dictionary* relates boredom to malaise, close to the French word *ennui,* which, as we have seen, means "to annoy." The French word comes from the Latin *inodiare,* which is even stronger as it means "to hold in hatred." It is an experience of weariness and dissatisfaction issuing from inactivity or lack of interest. It is a heavy cloud that hangs over everything or a murky lens through which each day is viewed. As a person who completed one of my surveys wrote, "My life was the same every day—getting up in the morning, going to work, doing work that I didn't like, coming home, taking a shower, eating, going to bed." There is an existential perception of life's futility, a deep sense of meaninglessness and purposelessness.

In both types of boredom there is a distortion of time—it seems to stand still. The German word for boredom, *langeweile*, literally means a "long time." Others refer to the experience of "an endless present."[1]

The poet Joseph Brodsky contrasts the two types of boredom rather dramatically: "The worst monotonous drone coming from a lectern or the most eye-splitting textbook written in turgid English is nothing in comparison to the psychological Sahara that starts right in your bedroom and spurns the horizon."[2] Jan Burte and Daniel Araoz reflect on this "paralysis of the soul" as they describe the symptoms of boredom as being

> encapsulated in a "So what?" attitude. Nothing excites or surprises the bored individual. The sense of awe is gone. Life has become plastic, mechanical, artificial. The bored person goes through life fulfilling obligations, often doing what is expected very well but in a robotized manner. Detachment, insensitivity, indolence, and apathy describe the bored person's life transactions. The poetic is absent. The bored person has become disconnected from savoring life's beauty.[3]

Martha Hyneman talks about the way T. S. Eliot wrote about sloth and boredom in that "great, tired poem, 'The Wasteland,' composed of the floating fragments of a fallen world." She relates it to the way some people go through life feeling "numb" and "blank," They "run every morning, cook, work, smile" and "make money," but inside they are "bankrupt" and empty.[4]

I described this state of mind earlier as an attitude in which there is nothing that one desires to do; in fact, there is an active desire not to do the activities that are available. Sometimes, it goes even beyond this. Seán Healy discusses the "pathological" boredom described by the psychoanalyst Otto Fenichel: "The problem then becomes not just the absence of a desired outlet for an impulse, or the presence of undesired ones, as in the 'normal' state, but the nagging desire for *something*, the nature of which is forever hidden."[5] Desire is not completely dead; it still longs for something.

In this second, deeper type of boredom there is a loss of passion for life and a lack of engagement in anything meaningful or satisfying, yet at the same time there is a longing for something more—something that is not satisfied by all the available opportunities.

Boredom is a feeling of "dullness and lack of vital interest in events or engagements."[6] It is a feeling of anxiety that an activity or situation has no meaning or purpose, which often drives the bored person to seek relief from the anxiety in a search for meaningful activity.

Some have likened the first type of boredom to seasickness: it is very uncomfortable while it lasts, but it is soon over when the cause is removed. The second type of boredom, however, is more like a chronic, painful and sometimes fatal disease.

Some people never seem to get bored. They are always active and interested in what they are doing. They may have multiple activities they enjoy and do well. Others seem to be bored much of the time. They struggle to find things to do when they are not working, and even when at work they do not engage very deeply in what they are doing. We will see that some of this difference is a result of temperament and some is a result of habitual attitudes and choices. One young woman wrote on a survey, "I find I quickly lose interest in different tasks once I have got over the challenge of learning what I have to do. I get disillusioned and bored with the monotony of daily life."

ANOTHER HISTORY LESSON—BUT A SHORT ONE!

Patricia Spacks demonstrates how references to boredom multiply astonishingly from the eighteenth to the twentieth centuries. She shows, in fascinating detail, how much English literature from the eighteenth and nineteenth centuries revolves around the theme of the boring nature of the lives of middle- to upper-class women.[7] Dickens was probably the first to use it in *Bleak House*, where Lady Dedlock endures the "chronic malady of boredom."[8] One of George Eliot's characters complains: "We are brought up like the flowers, to look as pretty as we can, and be dull without complaining. That is my notion about the plants: they are often bored, and that is the reason why some of them have got poisonous."[9] One of Fyodor Dostoevsky's characters in *The Possessed* pours out his nihilistic view of life: "I was so utterly bored that I could have hanged myself," he confesses, "and if I didn't, it was because I was still looking forward to something, as I have all my life. . . . Life bored me to the point of stupefaction."[10] More recently, Evelyn Waugh described the emptiness and boredom of the lives of the Bright Young People and their "Masked parties, Savage parties, Victorian parties . . . dull dances in London and comic dances in Scotland and disgusting dances in Paris—all that succession and repetition of massed humanity. . . . Those vile bodies."[11]

Approaching our own times, we find that contemporary novelists often focus on boredom. For example, in *Humboldt's Gift*, Saul Bellow invents a first-person narrator who is planning to write a book about "great bores of the modern world."[12] Anita Brookner's novels are "concerned with the lives of more or less isolated women for whom boredom is the assumed ground of experience."[13] One reviewer writes this of Walker Percy's characters: "For Percy, the typical alienated man is not some half-starving, half-crazed student out of a novel by Dostoyevsky or Sartre, but precisely the well-fed, successful, middle-class man or woman who seemingly 'has it all' and yet feels totally bored and empty."[14]

Contemporary rock songs also carry this theme of dissatisfaction and emptiness, which is often associated with boredom. The Rolling Stones had a past hit with "(I Can't Get No) Satisfaction." U2 sang "I Still Haven't Found What I'm Looking For" and later "Numb." Dave Matthews describes eating, drinking and wanting too much in the song "Too Much." The Buzzcocks have a song titled "Boredom" on their recent album *Time's Up*. The punk band Meanwhile sings "Boredom on Repeat" and "Life Is Hollow." Merril Bainbridge performs "Being Bored," and Far has a song called "Boring Life." Nirvana's bestselling "Smells Like Teen Spirit" demonstrates these themes as well. Some music critics call this preoccupation with life's meaninglessness "angst and roll" music.[15]

One need not dig too deep to find descriptions of a chronic restlessness and boredom emerging in literature, music, theater and movies. These expressions reflect the struggle in which we are all engaged: to find meaning and purpose in the daily routines and the necessary repetitions and duties of life.

But is it possible that the increase in boredom in recent years is due in part not to understimulation but to just the opposite—overstimulation? Most of us have more formal leisure hours to fill than those of previous generations, and the modern entertainment industry is not slow to fill our days with endless opportunities for distraction, as we will see in chapter four.

4

ENTERTAINED TO EXCESS

Leisure, Overstimulation and the Entertainment Industry

IN THE LAST CENTURY AND A HALF the number of hours Americans work per week has decreased dramatically while the number of hours available for leisure activities has increased. In the mid 1800s the average work week in America was approximately seventy hours, or the equivalent of six twelve-hour days, per week. At the turn of the last century, this figure came down to sixty hours per week. Before the Great Depression of 1929, fifty hours was the expected norm, and now many people expect to work little more than forty hours per week. Writes Robert Lee:

> It is a striking fact to note that the working man of a century ago spent some seventy hours per week on the job and lived about forty years. Today he spends some forty hours per week at work and can expect to live about seventy years. This adds something like twenty-two more *years of leisure* to his life, about 1,500 free hours each year, and a total of some 33,000 additional free hours that the man born today has to enjoy![1]

Since the Industrial Revolution there has been increasing separation of work and leisure. Prior to that time, these activities were often intermingled. For example, think of the move from rural farming to an industrial urban life: on the farm three generations of a family might can or bottle fruit together, working long hours but entertaining each other with songs and stories. Psychologist Mary Pipher describes such a lifestyle:

> The family was the source of everything. Anything that needed to be done
> was done by the family—fixing equipment, curing meat, treating illnesses in
> people or animals, mending harnesses and building furniture. There was al-
> ways work—gathering eggs, gardening, fixing fences, cleaning, planting, har-
> vesting and washing. Water was pumped and carried by hand. Butchering was
> in the fall, when the weather was cold enough to cool the meat. The family
> was up before dawn to milk the cows. In winter they hauled snow and buried
> it deep in the ground so that it would last into the summer. . . . The work
> made sense and produced concrete results.[2]

Life was hard, but after a day's work the family members might sit together talking or making music. The majority of the population would either stay at home or go to the local pub to drink, play cards and talk with
friends. They could escape into their own stories, but these settings usually
involved contact and communication with real people rather than escape
into the isolating fantasy world of a movie or television.

A friend of mine, who moved from the south of England to live on a
small farm on the island of Lewis in the Outer Hebrides (to the west of Scotland), wrote to me that

> [Pipher's] quote describes life on Lewis with animals, building to do, peat to
> dig, etc. I have found it so hard to watch television since moving here, as ar-
> tificial means of entertainment seem so dull in comparison with the hard
> work on the croft. Artificial entertainment seems irritating and trivial when
> you have to live so close to reality.

The recent PBS documentary *Frontier House* filmed three family groups
who lived for six months in the lifestyle of early frontier settlers in 1883 in
Montana. Through the spring, summer and fall of 2001 they were observed
as they built their houses, planted food, tended livestock and caught fish in
the stream, all without the help of modern technology. One family was interviewed after their return from the Montana cabin to their Malibu man-
sion. One of the children was having a hard time adjusting to a life where
basic needs are met so much more easily. She said, "Life in 2000 is boring.
Where's the fun in going to the mall every day?"[3]

RETREAT FROM COMMUNITY

I live in the city of St. Louis. I come home from work and occasionally wave to my neighbors and their children, greeting them with a friendly "Hi, how are you?" If I had a garage I would probably drive into it and enter the house from there without even seeing my neighbors. Most of us have all the entertainment we need in our home: television, computer, Internet, videos, music. A few of the older folk on my street sit out on their porches and chat with other older neighbors. The younger ones are too busy running to and from work, soccer games and school. And of course air-conditioning makes it unnecessary for us to seek the cooler breezes on the front porch. Pipher comments that "by 1990, 72 percent of Americans didn't know their neighbors."[4]

Rarely do families today sit down together for a meal, and when they do, the television is usually on in the background. Even more rarely do families get together to make music or play games.

Professor Michael Kammen claims that most leisure activities in the early twentieth century were participatory and interactive. For example, the sale of sheet music, which presumed a piano player and other musicians or singers, was a very important industry. After the recording industry took off in the 1920s, musical skill was no longer required because most people sat and listened to music rather than participating in making music themselves. He comments that even the radio requires some engagement of the listener's imagination; listening to radio is an activity sort of halfway between passivity and participation. But with the advent of television in 1948, little was left to the imagination, and in the 1970s the apt term "couch potato" was introduced into our language. Now the average American adult watches four to five hours of television a day, the average child watches three hours, and the television is turned on in the average American household for seven hours and forty minutes each day.[5] Geoffrey Godbey and John Robinson, in their studies of how Americans use time, found that average leisure time grew from about thirty-four hours in 1965 to about forty hours in 1985. How do we use most of that extra time? We watch television.[6]

Philosopher Roger Scruton, in a chapter titled "Yoofanasia," describes a contemporary youth culture that is cut off from the real world of respon-

sibilities and relationships with all ages in a broader family, political and religious community and that has its own pop subculture of entertainment
and diversion:

> Television has confined each young person from childhood onwards before a
> box of intriguing platitudes. Without speaking, acting or making himself in-
> teresting to others, he nevertheless receives a full quota of distractions. The
> TV provides a common and facile subject of communication, while extin-
> guishing the ability to communicate. The result is a new kind of isolation,
> which is as strongly felt in company as when alone.[7]

Author Wendell Berry laments the takeover of technology in *What Are
People For?*

> There used to be a sort of institution in our part of the country known as "sit-
> ting till bedtime." After supper, when they weren't too tired, neighbors
> would walk across the fields to visit each other. They popped corn, my friend
> said, and ate apples and talked. They told each other stories . . . about each
> other, about themselves, living again in their own memories and thus keeping
> their memories alive. . . .
>
> But most of us no longer talk with each other, much less tell each other
> stories. We tell our stories now mostly to doctors or lawyers or psychiatrists
> or insurance adjusters or the police, not to our neighbors for their (and our)
> entertainment. The stories that now entertain us are made up for us in New
> York or Los Angeles or other centers of such commerce.[8]

Today most people live in the very different world of urban technology
and industry, a world where so much is happening that it is hard keep up
and make sense of it all. With so many technological advances there is much
that is useful, and our lives are more comfortable for it. Boundaries between
work and leisure are much clearer, and a working week of forty to sixty
hours still leaves time in the evenings, weekends, public holidays and vacations for other things. This, however, is both a blessing and a curse. Increased leisure time can be very enjoyable if one has many interests, but it
also gives one more time in which to be bored, and because we are no longer
able to entertain ourselves we rely on the eager entertainment industry to
provide it for us. Bernard Shaw was probably thinking of the problem of lei-

sure when he wrote his definition of hell: "Hell is an endless holiday—the everlasting state of having nothing to do and plenty of money to spend on doing it."[9] The entertainment industry has responded to this need to the point of overstimulation. Robert Lee pushes this even further: "One often hears it said about a particularly active person that he died from overwork. With the shifting focus from work to leisure, is it possible that men now die of boredom, that they die from overleisure?"[10]

OVERSTIMULATED BY ENTERTAINMENT

When stimulation comes at us from every side, we reach a point where we cannot respond with much depth to anything. Bombarded with so much that is exciting and demands our attention, we tend to become unable to discriminate and choose from among the many options. The result is that we shut down our attention to everything. The boredom that we feel today is probably more likely to come from overload than underload. When we are surrounded by so much information, we find it hard to sort out what is relevant and important and to find meaning in anything.

In an essay on the quality of life in the information society, Orrin Klapp says that

> such a picture of overload dismisses the notion common among urbanites that boredom is mostly a problem of small towns, rural backwaters, or traditional societies outside the mainstream of progress. For all the allure of bright lights, the city has its own sorts of boredom. There is no evidence that people yawn more in small communities than in big ones.[11]

I certainly have plenty to do, and it would seem impossible that I should be bored in these circumstances. Each day I have to face information coming to me via ordinary "snail mail," e-mail, voice mail, telephone, Internet, radio and television. As I drive along the streets, billboards try to persuade me to drink a certain type of beer, to buy insurance from a particular company or to believe the local casino is the "road to entertainment." At airports and in planes it is hard to avoid constant video entertainment. When I stopped at one gas station, I was amazed to find a small video screen at each pump.

Georg Simmel, a sociologist, wrote in the 1950s of "the overload of sensations in the urban world, causing city dwellers to become jaded and develop a kind of psychic callus, the blasé attitude, 'an incapacity . . . to react to new situations with the appropriate energy.' "[12] A callus is a form of the body's self-defense against too much stimulation—a thickening and hardening of the normally sensitive skin. Boredom could be the psychological manifestation of an inner defense mechanism.

For some, escaping from an overload of information is a subconscious experience; for others, it is a deliberate and conscious choice. Ironically, some people seem to delight in boredom as an escape from the frenetic pace of contemporary urban life! As Patricia Spacks writes:

> An unknown woman approached me at a cocktail party. She wanted to know what I was writing these days. When I told her, she exclaimed, "Oh, I *love* to be bored!" Pressed to elaborate, she maintained that she always sought out boring movies, she looked for the most boring person at every party ("Thanks a lot," I said!), she treasured boring books. Boredom, she insisted, was the best escape from anxiety. It filled the mind; it kept worse things away. . . .
> As Joannie says in Gary Trudeau's *Doonesbury* (August 7, 1992), "Boredom? I would *welcome* boredom! I would *love* my life to be less interesting!"[13]

Some people give themselves over to boredom and make a lifestyle out of it! There is even a Boring Institute and a Dull Men's website. The "dull men" enjoy collecting dull trivia to share at dinner parties. Here are a few gems: When Heinz ketchup leaves the bottle, it travels at a rate of twenty-five miles per year. The only fifteen-letter word that can be spelled without repeating a letter is *uncopyrightable*. There are an average of 178 sesame seeds on a McDonald's McBun. All collected, the world's termites outweigh the world's humans ten to one. And then there is website Planet Boredom, "a gathering place for all the poor souls out there with nothing better to do."[14]

THE ENTERTAINMENT INDUSTRY

Overstimulation is felt most in relation to the entertainment and advertising industries. Instead of making our own entertainment, we now rely on radio, television and movies to entertain us. Of course entertainment is sometimes a good and necessary thing in moderation, but we are surrounded by constant stimulation. We do not have to work for it or put much effort into learning a new skill or area of interest. We can be passive couch potatoes and let it all come to us. And what comes to us is designed to grab our attention and get high ratings or reviews by being exciting, stimulating and entertaining.

William Wordsworth noted in the nineteenth century that some people had a "degrading thirst after outrageous stimulation."[15] Neal Gabler demonstrates how entertainment has become the primary measure of value: every experience has to be highly entertaining.[16] He suggests that human beings have always desired stimulation of their senses and that American culture, even in the nineteenth century, cultivated the sensational as a reaction against the artistic and intellectual elite; this sensationalism was a rebellion against the refined culture of Europe. The mass culture created by the entertainment industry in America now creates a fantasy world in which we aspire to live. The media create expectations for us, so ordinary life seems increasingly boring and we grow more dissatisfied. Thus we crave more of the media's sensational entertainment.

One of our most powerful contemporary and popular cultural critics, Bill Watterson, reflects on some of these themes in his cartoon, *Calvin and Hobbes*. Here's an example:

Calvin: "Popular culture isn't to blame for selling twisted values. Movies, records, and TV shows reflect the reality of our times. Artists depict hatred and violence because that's what they see."

Hobbes: "Why don't they see things of beauty and value?"

Calvin: "Because boring stuff doesn't sell."

Hobbes: "Such vision and integrity."

Calvin: "There's nothing like a good gunfight to uplift the spirit."[17]

Notice also in this example the theme that to the contemporary mind, goodness and beauty often seem boring and unstimulating. Goodness and beauty do not provide the adrenaline or testosterone rush produced by violence or sex! Many teenagers attempt to frighten themselves with horror movies such as *Friday the Thirteenth* or *Scream*. I am amazed (and appalled) by the radio pornography—aired at peak listening time for older teens and young adults here in St. Louis—on the *Howard Stern Show*. Sexuality of many varieties is graphically described, and people are often demeaned and made fun of—all for the sake, so Stern tells us, of being "titillating, exciting and funny."

ELECTRONIC GAMES

Video and computer games are a mixed blessing. They are certainly useful for entertaining children on a long car or plane journey. In June 2001, *Time* magazine's special computer supplement claimed that 60 percent of Americans play video games. It is surprising that they claim that the age of the typical gamer is not fourteen years old but twenty-eight years old, and that nearly half the game players are women. Lev Grossman writes:

> It's not every day that a new mass medium is born, but over the past decade America has seen video games not only emerge, but teethe, go through a moody adolescence and finally come of age. "I'm convinced games are a powerful art form in the process of finding its voice," says M.I.T. professor Henry Jenkins. "They're telling stories more and more deeply and communicating more and more profound ideas about everyday life."[18]

The better and more creative games allow the player to explore the consequences of his or her actions. A game can be replayed multiple times, experimenting with different plots and stories. The popular Sims series allows players to create and run their own imaginary society, full of characters who need help to live.

Some argue that video games destroy community because people spend hours alone at home playing them and become increasingly detached from real community. Others argue that it can create a new form of community because some games are competitive and are played online with friends. One family, living in different parts of the United States and separated by thousands of miles, gets together online every night to play cribbage and Microsoft's *Combat Flight Simulator*. In contrast to television programming, which is ingested by a passive audience, interactive computer games like *Sim City*, *Civilization II* and *Legend of Zelda* require players to participate and to develop strategic skills.

But there are real problems of addiction and isolation. Ten-year-old boys spend an average of nine and a half hours each week playing video games. Certainly, some games are good and creative, stretching players' skill and imagination, but other games are violent and pornographic. One woman wrote in response to a *Time* magazine article on computer games, "I do not believe that Internet Fantasy games like EverQuest can ever be harmless family fun. My husband invests so much of his time in his fantasy character that if it were his real-life character, he would have five graduate degrees by now."[19]

Craig A. Anderson, a psychology professor at Iowa State, recently testified before a U.S. Senate committee that video games can influence users more than television or movies can. He suggests that parents watch the games their kids are playing rather than relying on the title or rating printed on the box. A racing game might seem to be benign, he warns, but in some, the object is to run people over.[20] And now a new problem is emerging: in some games it will soon be difficult to differentiate real people online from computer-generated virtual actors.

EXTREME SPORTS

In *Outside* magazine, one professional skydiver and sky-surfer is quoted as saying, "It is only when my body is screaming toward Earth that I feel most truly alive."[21] Another said, "We're seen as people with a death wish, when actually we have a life wish: We want to experience as much as we can."[22] A climber who specializes in scaling vertical mountain cliffs "finds the vertical life extremely addictive" and says "we have a hard time dealing with the mundane. . . . Goals in ordinary life are never as pure or powerful as a big wall."[23] Research shows a significant relationship between the sensation-seeking temperament and the tendency to be bored.[24]

Previous generations of Americans and Europeans sought the ultimate challenges and experiences of living on the edge in the exploration of frontiers and wilderness, but now many of these once-impossible-to-reach places are open to tourists. Others experienced the challenge, excitement and terror of war. Bernard Moitessier, after fighting for the French army in Vietnam, said, "I learned to recognize the enormous rush you get in the Great Game of War, a kind of total alertness throughout your whole being, a heightened state."[25] Teen violence is increasing and gangs are never far from the news, but thankfully the majority of today's young people seek excitement in more peaceful pursuits. Yet many still hanker after some ultimate challenge. Karl Greenfield, writing in *Time* magazine on "why we take risks," said:

> Heading into the millennium, America has embarked on a national orgy of thrill seeking and risk taking. The rise of adventure and extreme sports like BASE jumping, snowboarding, ice climbing, skateboarding and paragliding is merely the most vivid manifestation of this new national behavior. Investors once content to buy stocks and hold them quit their day jobs to become day traders, making volatile careers of risk taking. Even our social behavior has tilted toward the treacherous, with unprotected sex on the upswing and hard drugs like heroin the choice of the chic as well as the junkies. In ways many of us take for granted, we engage in risks our parents would have shunned and our grandparents would have dismissed as just plain stupid.[26]

Sensation seeking in extreme sports has a respectability, but it is closely related to less reputable forms of entertainment and risk taking such as compulsive gambling, reckless driving, drug addiction, sexual addiction and violent criminality.

Temple University psychologist Frank Farley identifies people who crave excitement and new experiences as "Type T" personalities. He divides them into two groups: "intellectuals" (e.g., Albert Einstein and Pablo Picasso) and "physicals." The "Type T positive physicals" are the extreme-sports fanatics who indulge, for example, in free solo climbing without safety ropes or protective hardware; the negative Type T physicals are, for example, the bar-room brawlers. It is possible that those who have experiences of this sort (experiences pleasurable enough to compel them to engage in the activity again and again) have levels of brain chemicals and fear thresholds that are different from the average mortal's. There is evidence suggesting that three neurotransmitters—dopamine, which is associated with intense pleasure; serotonin, which is linked with different forms of extreme behavior; and norepinephrine, which is connected to the "fight or flight" response—are connected to sensation seeking and risk taking.[27]

In peacetime, Moitessier and a few other extraordinary men and women take on one of the most awesome challenges left on the globe: the single-handed, nonstop around-the-world sailing race (Vendée Globe). Imagine four months alone at sea in a sixty-foot racing machine. Several weeks of that time is spent in the Southern Ocean with huge waves, icebergs, fog, snow and the "unrelenting stress of storm after storm."[28] And all of this happens several days away from rescue if the boat capsizes or runs into other serious trouble. The race was created "to answer the needs of sailors eager to reach their uttermost limits."[29] Derek Lundy, in his book *Godforsaken Sea*, describes the stresses that these sailors experience:

> Non-sailors might try to visualize a never-ending series of five- or six-story buildings, with sloping sides of various angles and with occasional buildings half as high again, moving toward them at about forty miles an hour. Some of the time, the top one or two stories of the buildings will collapse on top of them. The concussive effect of seawater isn't much different from that of concrete. Add the isolation and the noise—the boom and roar of the waves, the deafening, unearthly, unnerving scream of wind around the obstructions of mast and rigging—and the picture should become clearer.[30]

Perhaps these men and women have nervous systems so different from our own that they feel less fear and need much more stimulation to feel pleasure and to feel alive. As Lundy comments, "Perhaps the Vendée Globe and Around Alone professional sailors tend to have large dopamine-receptor genes. Maybe it takes the Southern Ocean to squeeze enough chemical into their receptors to give them that nice natural high."[31] I find extreme pleasure—and, when fog or storms come, enough fear—just sailing in the English Channel or among the islands off the coast of Maine.

Most people do not have the opportunity, money or skill to sail the southern ocean or climb vertical mountains, so they have to find their adrenaline rush in some simple sport or perhaps at a horror movie.

The increasing interest in the extremes of abnormal behavior is seen in the voyeurism made available by the *Jerry Springer Show* or in some reality TV where people are humiliated in increasingly bizarre ways in front of the world. I have already mentioned the *Howard Stern Show*'s extreme efforts to shock, excite and attract attention. "On one episode of Spy TV," writes Michael Gordon, "people ate what they believed to be human flesh so that they could make it on to a reality TV program."[32] Shows such as *America's Funniest Home Videos, Frontier House* and *Survivor* are mostly harmless entertainment, but some extreme forms of reality TV like *Temptation Island* and *Fear Factor* are more akin to emotional pornography or "voyeur-vision" because of the pleasure obtained by watching other people in intimate emotional and physical situations. We are drawn in to intimate experiences without any responsibility or real relationship (compare sexual pornography) with the characters. People who love reality TV may live more intensely through the TV screen than they do in real life, face-to-face relationships.[33] Perhaps reality TV is so popular because it is feeding a deep hunger for two things that are lacking in my people's lives—intimacy and emotional authenticity.[34]

ORDINARY ENTERTAINMENT

Those of us who do not hunger for such extreme stimulation can still find plenty of entertainment in the endless shopping malls, restaurants, fitness clubs, tennis clubs, golf courses, gambling casinos, porn shops, strip clubs, movie theaters and late night television. This is the world of the big M's: the Mall, McDonald's and MTV.

In *Amusing Ourselves to Death*, Neil Postman quotes Robert MacNeil, former executive editor and co-anchor of the *MacNeil-Lehrer Newshour*, writing about the news:

> The idea, he writes, "is to keep everything brief, not to strain the attention of anyone but instead to provide constant stimulation through variety, novelty, action, and movement. You are required . . . to pay attention to *no* concept, no situation, no scene, no character, and no problem for more than a few seconds at a time."[35]

Ironically, because of the media's ability to communicate extraordinary events in such dramatic ways, the daily round of our rather humdrum lives seems more boring. And we must note in passing that the word *amuse* comes from the French word *amuser*, which means "to stare fixedly"! The most common amusement and entertainment is found as we stare at a screen.

With the availability of cable and satellite television, we have literally hundreds of channels to surf. If ever there was a symbol of the present times, channel surfing is it. The mind is excited by the endless possibilities of surfing the Web or even surfing the waves, always waiting and hoping for the bigger and better thrill. Professor Gene Veith writes, "Boredom is a chronic symptom of a pleasure-obsessed age. When pleasure becomes one's number one priority, the result, ironically, is boredom."[36] Author Henry Fairlie comments on sloth, saying, "So we whiffle away our lives, with no real purpose or strenuousness. Who's for tennis? In at least its courts, we will serve. We will ride to paradise on a golf cart."[37]

Inner resources to cope with potentially boring and threatening situations are depleted when one is malnourished by a constant diet of entertainment. Only in certain unusual and unexpected circumstances do our addiction to entertainment and the depletion of our inner resources become noticeable. In the chapter one, we contemplated the consequences of a prolonged power failure in which all electronic devices would be lying dormant and unusable. T. S. Eliot catches one such poignant experience:

> Or as, when an underground train, in the tube, stops too long between stations
>> And the conversation rises and slowly fades into silence
>> And you see behind every face the mental emptiness deepen
>> Leaving only the growing terror of nothing to think about.[38]

The terror lies in the realization that there might be nothing with which to perpetuate the self-induced process of being "distracted from distraction by distraction."[39] But as we will see, there are plenty of people anxious to catch our attention, eager to fill the vacuum of our leisure hours and to help us to relieve any traces of boredom.

5

ADVERTISED TO APATHY

The Stimulation and Disappointment of Desire

IT IS HARD FOR US TO IMAGINE A WORLD without advertising. Advertising has always existed in some form, but the industry as we know it today began with the great international expositions and world's fairs initiated in London, at the Crystal Palace, in 1851. This was followed by expositions in Paris, Chicago, St. Louis and other cities at the turn of the century. The organizers of these huge, extraordinary fairs intended for them to educate, entertain and, of course, to celebrate and sell the latest technological innovations and means of production. Great buildings were constructed to house the grand exhibits and to give space for lavish displays of the exotic cultures and merchandise of the African and Far Eastern countries. Fountains, lakes, hills, towers (e.g., the Eiffel Tower in 1889) and giant Ferris wheels (e.g., in St. Louis in 1904) were built. By the early 1900s "expositions and fairs had become miniature cities of consumption, whose utopian rhetoric was that each consumable object contained within itself the power of bliss."[1]

Another force in the spread of consumerism at that time was the advent of the department store. Built in 1869, the Bon Marché in Paris was

> enormous and its architecture histrionic; it had the appearance of a theater and even at times of a temple. . . .

Displays in the various departments depicted the bourgeois life-styles. There were scenes of women wearing "coats for visit, coats for travel, coats for ball, or coats for the theatre." There were many family scenes as well: the family at the beach, in the countryside, at dinner. Children were not neglected, for there were entire departments devoted to their needs and life-style. The store's catalogues, calendars, and illustrated cards reinforced and added to the ideal image of bourgeois life that the various departments promoted: "The Bon Marché showed people how they should dress, how they should furnish their home, and how they should spend their leisure time."[2]

Then came the "uniquely American contribution to consumption"— the mail-order catalog. For those in the rural farming communities outside the big cities, the catalog was a necessary and helpful way to buy all they needed. Sears, Roebuck and Company was the largest mail-order company. Their catalog's circulation grew from over 300,000 in 1897 to over three million in 1907. Historian Daniel Boorstin comments on its status in many households at that time:

> It was not merely facetious to say that many farmers came to live more intimately with the good Big Book of Ward's or Sears, Roebuck than with the Good Book. The farmer kept his Bible in the frigid parlor, but as Edna Ferber remarked in *Fanny Herself* (1917), her novel of the mail-order business, the mail-order catalogue was kept in the cozy kitchen. That was where the farm family ate and where they really lived. For many such families the catalogue probably expressed their most vivid hopes of salvation.[3]

These descriptions of the department store and the place of the mail-order catalog in the life of most Americans sound remarkably contemporary. Many scholars believe that a major change in American life occurred between approximately 1870 and 1940, the years of the great world's fairs. This "second industrial revolution" is more often called the "consumer revolution" because in that time our culture changed from one in which people organized their lives around the process of production to one in which people were ruled by consumption. Professor Lendol Calder comments on the enormity of this change:

> This shift is Copernican in magnitude, being nothing less than the overthrow

of one world-picture (scarcity/work/community) for another (abundance/ leisure/self-fulfillment). In terms of its effects for everyday people, some say the consumer revolution can only be compared to what happened 8,000 years before Christ, when neolithic hunter-gatherers exchanged their spears for the plow.[4]

This development over the last 150 years has produced endless commercials, catalogs and credit-card solicitations that pour into our living rooms from the television, through our mailboxes or onto our computers via the Internet. A day rarely goes by in which we do not receive at least four or five catalogs in the mail. These commercials and catalogs show us the current fashions and styles that, we are led to believe, are essential for our sense of acceptance and identity among our peers as well as for our physical and psychological well-being. They are designed very specifically and carefully to stimulate dissatisfaction and boredom with what we already have. They want us to follow our appetites and desires. For example, did you notice the not-so-subtle change of slogan a few years ago in advertisements for Sprite soda from "I like the Sprite in you" to "Image is nothing. Thirst is everything. Obey your thirst"?

Patricia Spacks provides some other good examples. For instance, relieving boredom could become very expensive if the following advertisement is true: "Fly the Concorde around the world. The future way to fly—NOW. Everything else is boring."[5] Such commercials can exist only in a culture of material affluence. One social scientist comments that

> affluence provides the freedom from necessity and its attendant intense activity that allows the pressing ache of boredom to emerge into awareness. It is not affluence that causes boredom, it only creates the conditions in which the long-present boredom becomes experienced.[6]

Somewhat more mundane is this commercial for fountain pens:

> A sexy woman lolls on a Directoire chaise. "I gave up chocolates," the copy reads. "I gave up espresso. I gave up the Count (that naughty man). And his little house on Cap Ferrat. The Waterman, however, is not negotiable. I must have something thrilling with which to record my boredom."[7]

THIRSTY IN THE RAIN

Boorstin writes of advertising as the "omnipresent, most characteristic, and most remunerative form of American literature." It was "destined to have an intimate popular appeal and a gross national influence without parallel in the history of sacred and profane letters."[8]

What does the advertising industry do to you? It wants its endless commercials and catalogs to breed in you dissatisfaction and discontent with your house, your car, your body, your clothes—in other words, to stimulate in you a desire for more than you have. In old-fashioned biblical language it inspires you to covet. It promises you satisfaction, peace, meaning and happiness, but only if you get your needs met now. Stivers writes:

> Advertising and the attendant mass media create a world of the eternal present, a world in which everything is constantly changing, a world in which our purpose as consumers is always to seek new experiences. . . . "Advertisements were [and are] *secular* sermons, exhortations to seek [fulfillment] through the consumption of material goods and mundane services."[9]

The entertainment industry—movies, videos, sports, commercials, television shows—elbows its way into your home. All your needs can be met, at least for a while: Hungry? Order a pizza. Bored? Rent a video. Lustful? . . . And for a while these things make us feel alive and satisfied, but soon the same desires resurface. Thomas Aquinas would have said that such people suffer from "a roaming unrest of spirit."[10]

Calvin is walking on the branch of a tree one day and says to his friend Hobbes, "Getting is better than having. When you *get* something, it's new and exciting. When you *have* something, you take it for granted and it's boring." Hobbes replies, "But everything you *get* turns into something you *have*." And Calvin responds, "That's why you always get new things!" "I feel like I'm in some stockholder's dream," says Hobbes. Calvin has the last word: " 'Waste and want,' that's *my* motto."[11]

Could it be that some have become so chronically disappointed by false promises and unfulfilled wants that they have shut down their deepest longings and desires and become apathetic and bored? The enticements to more exciting things have to get louder to catch our dulled attention. Some continue to pursue the dream of satisfaction held out by advertisers' promises, and when one fails another promise takes its place. But some people, frustrated by pursuing mirages and riding an emotional roller coaster, eventually lose interest and do not want to risk being disappointed again. They give up the hope and expectation that anything could ever give them deep pleasure. They become like the dwarves in C. S. Lewis's *The Last Battle* who are "so afraid of being taken in that they cannot be taken out."[12] They had become so cynical about the existence of goodness that when true deliverance was offered, they could not see the opportunity or beauty right in front of them.

One explanation for this phenomenon from a Christian perspective is found in the biblical description of end-state boredom that is found in the letter of Paul to the Ephesians. Paul describes people who have hardened their hearts against God: "Having lost all sensitivity, they have given themselves over to sensuality . . . with a continual lust for more" (Eph 4:19). He is describing the loss of true sensitivity and satisfaction in the many wonderful things that our Creator has given us to enjoy, such as a delicious meal, a fine wine, a walk in the woods in autumn, a beautiful piece of music, a stirring play or opera, an evening sail, a sunset or making love to your spouse. He is arguing that when we cut ourselves off from God we tend to look for our deepest fulfillment and meaning only in the things that God has made rather than in a relationship with him. The Bible describes this as a form of idolatry—worship of a false god—and Paul says that people who seek ultimate pleasure in, for example, food, art or sex will often pursue endless diversions and distractions as each one in turn becomes boring and dissatisfying. Mary Pipher observes:

> In the 1990s ironies abound. With more entertainment we are bored. With more sexual information and stimulation, we experience less sexual pleasure. In a culture focused on feelings, people grow emotionally numb. . . . We are (to quote Peter Rowan) "thirsty in the rain."[13]

DELAYED GRATIFICATION

It is estimated that by the age of twenty many young people have seen well over one million commercials. From advertisements, says Pipher, children learn that they are the most important person in the universe, that impulses should not be denied, that pain should not be tolerated and that the cure for any kind of pain is a product. They learn a weird mix of dissatisfaction and entitlement. With the messages of ads, we are socializing children to be self-centered, impulsive and addicted.[14]

Television does the opposite of encouraging delayed gratification. At the heart of the contemporary concept of "emotional intelligence" is this concept of delayed gratification. Emotional intelligence refers to one's capacity for relationships, one's sensitivity to oneself and others, and one's social and emotional skills. In an experiment at Stanford University known as the "marshmallow test," four-year-olds were brought into a room one by one. On the table in the room was a marshmallow. Each child was told, "You can have this marshmallow now if you want. But if you don't eat it until after I get back from running an errand, you can have two when I return."

Fourteen years later, at the time these children were graduating from high school, researchers compared the children who ate the marshmallow immediately with the children who waited and got two. Those who grabbed the marshmallow were (as eighteen-year-olds) more likely to fall apart under stress, had a tendency to become irritated and to pick fights more often, and were less able to resist temptation in pursuit of their goals. There was also a completely unanticipated and surprising finding in this comparison of the young adults: the SAT scores of the children who had waited were an average of 210 points higher (out of a possible 1600 points) than the scores of those who had not waited. By the time they reached their late twenties, the differences between these young adults were even more remarkable. Those who had shown greater self-control as four-year-olds were "more intellectually skilled, more attentive, and better able to concentrate. They were better able to develop genuine and close relationships, were more dependable and responsible, and showed better control in the face of frustration." The children who were more impulsive at four were now, in adulthood

less cognitively adept and strikingly less emotionally competent than those who had restrained themselves. They were more often loners, they were less dependable, more easily distracted, and unable to delay gratification in pursuing their goals. When stressed, they had little tolerance or self-control.

They responded to pressure with little flexibility, instead repeating the same futile and overblown response time and again.[15]

Could it be that commercials are more dangerous to a child's soul than are sex and violence, the things that make parents so anxious? The commercials teach self-indulgence and the right to instant gratification. Could it be that the media-centric environment in which our children grow up saturates them with entertainment, disconnects them from reality, and eventually numbs and deadens the sensibilities of their souls? Many other cultural critics are concerned about the effect of media on the next generation. A few years ago in an excellent article in *New Yorker* magazine titled "Buried Alive: Our Children and the Avalanche of Crud," David Denby wrote:

> The danger is not mere exposure to occasional violent or prurient images but the acceptance of a degraded environment that devalues everything—a shadow world in which our kids are breathing an awful lot of poison without knowing that there's clean air and sunshine elsewhere. They are shaped by the media as consumers before they've had a chance to develop their souls.

Denby vividly describes his son, glued to computer war games, videos and television on the weekends, ignoring plates of raw vegetables and fried chicken, and consuming junk food. He sees that his child does not stay interested in one thing for long but instead moves restlessly from one game or show to another.

> The endless electronic assault obviously leaves its marks all over him. The children grow up, but they become ironists, ironists of waste. They know that everything in the media is disposable. Everything on television is just for the moment—It's just television—and the kids pick up this devaluing tone, the sense that nothing matters.[16]

In a similar vein, Todd Gitlin reflects on "the weirdness of spending so many of our hours awash in the media." "I am concerned," he says, "with what media do in common—produce a habitat conducive to Feeling Lite, civic disengagement, and a national attention-deficit disorder."[17]

This oppression and subconscious brainwashing by television and the consumer and entertainment culture is much harder to recognize than is the tyrannical control of a dictator like Joseph Stalin, Adolf Hitler or Saddam Hussein. Neil Postman compares the two visions of the future: the depiction of a cruel and despotic government in George Orwell's *1984* and the depiction found in Aldous Huxley's *Brave New World:*

> What Huxley teaches is that in the age of advanced technology, spiritual devastation is more likely to come from an enemy with a smiling face than from one whose countenance exudes suspicion and hate. In the Huxleyan prophecy, Big Brother does not watch us, by his choice. We watch him, by ours.
>
> People will come to love their oppression, to adore the technologies that undo their capacities to think.[18]

I have been focusing on the negative aspects of the age in which we live. Of course much of technology (and the entertainment industry) is good. It has given us amazing freedom from disease and drudgery. It has given us some wonderful music, great movies and amazing video games in our homes. It has enabled us to travel and communicate around the globe with incredible efficiency and ease. But technology seems to act as a giant amplifier of both aspects of the world—all that is wonderful and good *and* all that is terrible and evil. Os Guinness, reflecting on sloth and boredom, describes another aspect of these two sides of modern life:

> We think of the rise of the modern world as the story of dynamism, energy, progress, and achievement—which it is. But we often overlook its other side. The world produced by such dynamism is a world of convenience, comfort, and consumerism. And when life is safe, easy, sanitized, climate-controlled, and plush, sloth is close.
>
> The flipside of dynamic optimism is corrosive boredom. . . . Equally the flipside of consumerism is complacency. The most compulsive of shoppers and channel-surfers move from feeling good to feeling nothing.[19]

In the last two chapters we have explored the culture of entertainment and advertising and its relationship to boredom. But there is an intriguing question that we have not yet addressed: Why is it that some people seem to be so much more prone to boredom than others? Is it a character defect, a problem of brain function or perhaps a psychological problem? We will try to answer this question next.

6

WHY SOME PEOPLE ARE
MORE LIKELY TO GET BORED

Perception, Personality and Proneness

"BOREDOM IS ALSO IN THE EYE OF THE BEHOLDER," writes Peter Conrad. "What may be boring to one person may be fascinating to another."[1]

An artist friend of mine told me of a time when he was drawing pictures of men at work in an automobile construction plant in Canada. One of the subjects was a man who, for eight hours a day, operated a machine that inserted bolts into a part of each car on the assembly line. During one of his breaks, the man wandered over to watch the artist at work. My friend explained what he was doing, and the man turned away, saying, "Boy, some guy's got a boring job!" Boredom is not simply in the nature of the task but in each person's perception of the task.

I have learned that some students may find my class incredibly interesting and stimulating whereas others in the same class may find it boring and painful. Student perceptions may be influenced by whether or not they appreciate my teaching style. But their perceptions are also deeply affected by their temperament, life experiences, physical state (e.g., whether they are tired during an afternoon class) and their view of the topic's relevance to their life at that particular time.

PERSONALITY AND TEMPERAMENT

In the research literature a distinction is made between a state of boredom and a personality trait of boredom. A state of boredom is defined as "a state of relatively low arousal and dissatisfaction, which is attributed to an inadequately stimulating situation."[2] This state may be felt by anyone in a monotonous and repetitive situation. A personality trait of boredom is defined as "a tendency to experience tedium and lack of personal involvement and enthusiasm, to have a general or frequent lack of sufficient interest in one's life surrounding and future."[3] It seems that some people—whether because of brain structure, early life experiences or temperament—are more likely to experience boredom.

There are times in life when we actually should seek a lack of stimulation. It is important to have times of quiet and withdrawal from the frenetic business of life, times of lying on the beach, times of putting our feet up and doing nothing for a while or times of enjoying simple, uncomplicated, daily rituals. But this relaxing is particularly difficult for some people who find it very hard to be alone or to be still. Introverts tend to be happier with their own company and with quiet surroundings than do extroverts who need the stimulation of people and activity. Research has shown a consistent correlation between extroversion and the tendency to boredom.[4] Extroverts, more than introverts, find that monotony, repetition and understimulation produce discomfort, restlessness and a lack of perseverance in solving boring frustrating problems. In one simple study, students were given a difficult jigsaw puzzle to put together. The students who quit scored higher on extroversion.[5] In general, men have a significantly higher need for external stimulation as measured by an individual's need for challenge, excitement and variety. For the same reason, men also tend to score higher on the Boredom Proneness Scale.[6] People who have a high need to seek sensation and novelty are more likely to get bored. We have seen this already in reference to extreme sports.

There is also an association between a tendency to procrastinate and a proneness to boredom.[7] This could be a complex defense against not being able to do things perfectly, as there is also a connection between perfectionism and boredom. Retreating into procrastination and complaining of boredom with a task are both ways of escaping responsibility for completion of a task and thus avoiding the risk of failure or imperfection.

Many authors comment on the connection between boredom and the tendency to be self-focused and narcissistic. As one might expect, boredom is also associated with distractibility, low attention control and concentration difficulties. The phrases "intolerance of boredom" and "a restless search for stimulation" often appear on lists of the symptoms of Attention Deficit Hyperactivity Disorder (ADHD) in children and adults. There is much debate about the legitimacy of this diagnosis, with its central symptoms of inattention, impulsivity and hyperactivity. It is certainly very difficult to draw a clear line between personality and pathology. As I look at the current state of the evidence, I am persuaded that far too many prescriptions for Ritalin-like drugs are being prescribed for behavior problems that could be helped without medication. However, I am also persuaded that some people have a neurological problem that may be exacerbated by our fast-paced, demanding culture. These folk have many of the symptoms of ADHD or ADD (Attention Deficit Disorder without hyperactivity) and benefit significantly—sometimes dramatically—from medication.

Proneness to boredom is associated with higher ratings on all five scales of the Hopkins Symptom Checklist, a measure of mental health. The five scales are obsessive-compulsive, somatization (a tendency to express psychological tension in physical symptoms), anxiety, interpersonal sensitivity and depression.[8]

MEASURING BOREDOM

How can an experience like boredom be measured? The most commonly used scale measures the temperamental qualities of people who are more susceptible to boredom. The Boredom Proneness Scale has people answer twenty-eight true-false questions, given below.[9] When this test is administered it is usually done under the title "Experience of Activities," not "Boredom Proneness." Take the test yourself.

1. It is easy for me to concentrate on my activities.   *True or False*

2. Frequently when I am working I find myself
   worrying about other things.   *True or False*

3. Time always seems to be passing slowly.　　*True or False*

4. I often find myself at "loose ends,"
   not knowing what to do.　　*True or False*

5. I am often trapped in situations
   where I have to do meaningless things.　　*True or False*

6. Having to look at someone's home movies
   or travel slides bores me tremendously.　　*True or False*

7. I have projects in mind all the time, things to do.　　*True or False*

8. I find it easy to entertain myself.　　*True or False*

9. Many things I have to do are repetitive
   and monotonous.　　*True or False*

10. It takes more stimulation to get me going
    than most people.　　*True or False*

11. I get a kick out of most things I do.　　*True or False*

12. I am seldom excited about my work.　　*True or False*

13. In any situation I can usually find something
    to do or see to keep me interested.　　*True or False*

14. Much of the time I just sit around doing nothing.　　*True or False*

15. I am good at waiting patiently.　　*True or False*

16. I often find myself with nothing to do—
    time on my hands.　　*True or False*

17. In situations where I have to wait,
    such as a line or a queue, I get very restless.　　*True or False*

18. I often wake up with a new idea.　　*True or False*

19. It would be very hard for me to find a job
    that is exciting enough.　　*True or False*

20. I would like more challenging things to do in life.   *True or False*

21. I feel that I am working below my abilities
    most of the time.   *True or False*

22. Many people would say that I am a
    creative or imaginative person.   *True or False*

23. I have so many interests, I don't have
    time to do everything.   *True or False*

24. Among my friends, I am the one who keeps
    doing something the longest.   *True or False*

25. Unless I am doing something exciting,
    even dangerous, I feel half-dead and dull.   *True or False*

26. It takes a lot of change and variety
    to keep me really happy.   *True or False*

27. It seems that the same things are on television
    or the movies all the time; it's getting old.   *True or False*

28. When I was young, I was often in
    monotonous and tiring situations.   *True or False*

Answers indicating a susceptibility to boredom: False: 1, 7, 8, 11, 13, 15, 18, 22, 23, 24. True: 2, 3, 4, 5, 6, 9, 10, 12, 14, 16, 17, 19, 20, 21, 25, 26, 27, 28. Each answer indicating boredom is worth one point. A score of 0-5 = low boredom proneness; a score of 15-28 = high boredom proneness.

Analysis of this test in different groups of people shows that boredom may be a function of five factors.[10] The first is the "need for external stimulation": excitement, challenge and often change in activities such as channel- or Web-surfing, or the adrenaline rush of extreme sports. Marvin Zuckerman originally described sensation seeking as a personality trait where there is a "need for varied, novel, and complex sensations and experiences and the willingness to take physical and social risks for the sake of such experience."[11] In general, males tend to have greater sensation-seeking needs than females.[12] Zuckerman also distinguishes curiosity from sensation seeking.[13]

The second factor is the "capacity for internal stimulation," keeping oneself interested and entertained. Some people seem to have greater inner resources for dealing with the inevitable tedium of some parts of life. We see this capacity in some very young children who seem to be so much better at entertaining themselves than others; they will play for hours without needing interaction from parents or friends. One person wrote on my survey on boredom, "I find it very difficult to get bored. There is too much to think about, read about, write about, speak about, and hear about. Look, there is far too damn much to *learn* about." The very gifted and eccentric writer Cormac McCarthy said, "Everything is interesting. I don't think I have been bored for 50 years. I've forgotten what it was like."[14]

The third factor is the "affective response," a person's emotional reaction to boredom. One person may become irritated and restless; another will remain calm and patient. Think of the different ways in which people react to waiting in a long line at the checkout counter, for example. Another student wrote on my survey, " I get very bored with long-term baby sitting. Everyday having to be with the same children and playing their favorite game. It gets very boring always having to focus on pleasing them." I mentioned earlier other research which found that people who are focused on pleasing themselves probably experience greater boredom than those who focus more often on meeting the needs of others.

The fourth factor, "perception of time," relates to a person's organization and use of time, and perception of the passage of time. The subjective sense of boredom is closely correlated with a sense of time passing very slowly and there being "nothing to do," nothing that arouses sufficient interest. Those who never feel they have enough time to do all they have to do in life rarely experience boredom. As we say, "How time flies when you are having fun!"

The fifth factor, "constraint," is a measure of the ability to deal with constraining situations such as waiting in line, sitting in a boring class or traveling on a long journey in a bus or plane. When the sense of not being able to escape is strong, the boredom will be greater: "I get bored when I am longing to do one thing but am trapped doing another." In an experimental situation, when people were given repetitive tasks and asked to continue them beyond the point at which they wanted to stop, they experienced greater boredom.[15]

So according to the Boredom Proneness Scale, boredom is a function of several factors that are partly innate and partly learned. A person's inner needs, capacities and emotional reactions deeply affect how one responds to potentially boring situations.

It seems that there are certain personality characteristics that make some people more prone to boredom. How much of this is built-in or hard-wired (nature) and how much is a result of childhood influences (nurture) we do not know, but it does mean that some will have to work harder at maintaining interest in life than will others.

Research using the Boredom Proneness Scale has shown that people who are prone to boredom are also more likely to be more depressed, hopeless and lonely.[16] They are more likely to be impulsive and sensation seeking.[17] They tend to have more feelings of alienation, hostility and anxiety.[18] Those who have lower scores on this scale tend to have more life satisfaction and autonomy,[19] and they are happier and more assertive.[20] A study of psychosocial development in students showed that those with low boredom proneness had significantly higher scores on such scales as career planning, lifestyle planning, peer relationships, educational involvement, emotional autonomy, interdependence and academic autonomy.[21] In such studies, it is, of course, difficult to separate cause and effect.

With so many negative traits associated with proneness to boredom, it is challenging to find ways in which the greater restlessness and a desire for excitement can be channeled into creative pursuits and careers. People with such traits may seek out jobs that have great challenge, variety and perhaps danger: they may become construction workers, explorers, war photographers or even pioneer surgeons!

THE YAWN FACTOR

If we were to play a simple word-association game, I am sure that the first word to come into most people's minds in relation to *boredom* would be *yawn*. We cannot leave our brief reflection on the measurement and scientific analysis of boredom without considering the fascinating and familiar link between boredom and yawning.

We usually consider yawning in social situations to be rude. Yawning signifies boredom, fatigue or drowsiness. When someone is watching us, we try to stifle such yawns. Several years ago Robert Provine studied the basic features of the common yawn and discovered that the average yawn lasted six seconds with a range of four to eleven seconds![22] When sitting alone in a cubicle for half an hour and having been instructed to think about yawning, subjects of his study yawned an average of twenty-eight times, with the highest number of yawns being seventy-six and the lowest being one. Provine was able to repeat the experiment three weeks later and obtained the same results. He also found when his subjects watched videotape of people yawning or read about yawning, the incidence of yawns increased. You may find yourself yawning now! The frequency of yawns is greatest in the hour after waking and the hour before going to bed. The number of yawns also tends to increase a little in the early afternoon, when many people feel sleepy for a while.

Using twenty-eight psychology students as subjects, researchers found that the most frequent activities during which subjects yawned were (in order of frequency) sitting in class, driving a car, studying and reading, and watching television.[23] Students in lecture classes yawn at a much higher rate than those in aerobics classes, dining halls or libraries.[24] As one might expect, more frequent yawning is associated with viewing uninteresting, repetitive stimuli than with viewing interesting stimuli.[25] Researchers believe that yawning occurs at a transition between levels of arousal in the brain, and it seems to help to keep the central nervous system aroused in situations where attention is important but the environment is relatively unstimulating. Newborn babies "yawn a few minutes after taking their first breath,"[26] and a twenty-week-old fetus has even been observed yawning in the womb! "During their first year of school," writes Ronald Baenninger, "children yawn five times as frequently as they did in nursery school."[27] Given the constraints of the relatively sedentary school classroom, with its lower levels of stimulation and movement, students may need other mechanisms to keep their brains aroused. Perhaps their brains have developed to a point where they need more stimulation.

A school or university classroom is one of the most likely places to find a lot of yawning, with the deadly combination of a boring, early afternoon lecture after a late-night party. Trying to stay awake on long car journeys is often punctuated by frequent yawning. Yawning somehow helps the brain to stay alert in any situation where sleep would be dangerous or embarrassing. It is commonly believed that yawning increases the oxygen supply to the brain, but there is little evidence that this is the case. So it seems that most spontaneous yawns have the function of stimulating the brain in a situation of tiredness or boredom. The highest incidence of yawns will be seen when these two conditions—tiredness and boredom—occur at the same time.[28]

Thus far I have described the phenomenon of boredom and both the personality traits and the social factors that contribute to it. We were lured for a few moments into the mouth of the yawn. Now we must turn to the world of psychology and psychotherapy, to an exploration of the thoughts and feelings that lie below the surface of conscious awareness.

7

NEGATED TO NUMBNESS

Anxiety, Disappointment and Emotional Shutdown

MANY PEOPLE ARE FRIGHTENED BY emotionally intense situations. Whether the feelings are of failure, inadequacy, sadness, frustration, anxiety, fear, disappointment or anger, such feelings may be deeply uncomfortable. If they cannot be expressed appropriately, they may be repressed into the unconscious or barely conscious places of the mind and heart. There they sit, waiting for some means of release. Some naturally inhibited or timid people or those who have learned by painful experience that expressing negative feelings is wrong will want to keep themselves safe at all costs. They may cut themselves off from the conscious awareness of most feelings and become somewhat numb to their inner reality. They may then experience this numbness as boredom with relationships, life and the world.

FAMILY DYSFUNCTION AND DEEP DISAPPOINTMENTS

"John" came to see me for psychotherapy because he was struggling with depression and boredom. He had experienced years of childhood criticism, neglect and abuse, and he made a half-conscious decision that "if no one delights in me, I will delight in nothing and nobody." In order to survive, he repressed his anger, grief and sadness. As he pushed down negative, painful feelings, he often buried positive ones too. Every child longs for love and affirmation. Repeated rejection, disappointment and hurt lead to a shutting down of deep desires and to a numbness of soul. John made a decision to avoid any risk of hurt or disappointment by resolving never to trust anyone deeply or hope for anything again. When feelings are repressed in this way, the world may be experienced as colorless and boring. All feelings, especially unpleasant ones, fall into the same mode of "shutdown"—and hence, boredom—and are never felt for what they really are.

Naomi was sexually abused by her uncle. As she worked through the pain of her abuse in therapy, she became acutely aware of her guilt and shame at having felt some pleasure in the sexual arousal. This pleasure was associated with enormous shame and guilt because as an eight-year-old, she sensed that there might be something wrong with what her uncle was doing. He told her how much he loved her. He gave her gifts and made her feel very special. He told her that she was very beautiful. She loved his attention and affection and did not know what was normal. With the pleasure, shame and guilt, she began to think of herself as a very bad person for having felt any pleasure at all. When she reached adolescence, in order to protect herself from these feelings, she shut down her desires and longings for close relationships with young men and became a very sweet and kind young woman, always wanting to please other people but with little heart and passion for life. In fact, life became boring as she disengaged from any deep relationships or pleasures. Dan Allender writes of this deep ambivalence felt by victims of sexual abuse: feeling the legitimate pleasure that God has designed us for and, at the same time, feeling associated shame and guilt. This intolerable conflict, of which victims are often only barely conscious, leads to dissociation from reality and a loss of passion for life.[1]

NUMBING OF THE SOUL

Numbed feelings may have other causes. People who have experienced life-threatening trauma in war, assault, rape or dangerous rescue missions such as those following earthquakes and hurricanes may suffer from what we call "posttraumatic stress disorder." For months and sometimes years, these people may experience depression, anxiety, suicidal thoughts and, underlying these, a fear of feeling too much emotion lest they be plunged back into the horror of the past trauma. They often lose interest in things that used to give them pleasure; they are wary of responding to calls for help when someone is in need. They are preoccupied with their own pain, longing to be free. One young man that I counseled worked in an AIDS hospice for two years, caring for men and women in extreme states of physical and mental deterioration. He watched more than seventy of them die. He found himself, several years later, depressed, suicidal, numb to most joy and pleasure in life and suffering from "compassion fatigue" and posttraumatic stress disorder.

We cannot live this way for long—desperately wanting to feel alive but not daring to risk relationships with people or even a God who may hurt us or disappoint us. Yet we may try other things that give the illusion of life and intimacy: pornography, sex, drugs, food, anything that will give a high, a moment of intense feeling, of ecstasy, of life. Ralph Greenson writes of boredom experienced as a feeling of emptiness.

> [It is] a combination of instinctual tension and a vague feeling of emptiness. The instinctual tension is without direction due to the inhibition of thoughts and fantasies. Tension and emptiness is felt as a kind of hunger—stimulus hunger. Since the individual does not know for what he is hungry, he now turns to the external world, with the hope that it will provide the missing aim and/or object.[2]

This pursuit can be dangerous because the tension is easily relieved for a while with alcohol, drugs or sex and the emptiness may be temporarily filled by food, a frenetic social life or a busy work schedule. We will consider this more when we look at the byproducts of boredom (see chapter eleven).

Boredom has been described as "a denial of one's soul."[3] Repressing emotion leads to an inner calm, but it comes at the price of losing many positive emotions as well: "The walls the boring client builds to keep safely in also keep excitement out."[4] Such a person may be very skilled at intellectually analyzing her life but find it very difficult to get in touch with her feelings. Child psychologist Bruno Bettleheim said, "Boredom was a sign of too many feelings, too deep and too hard to summon to the surface."[5]

A striking portrayal of cutting oneself off from uncomfortable feelings of guilt and anxiety is found in Albert Camus's novel *The Stranger*. The hero, when asked if he has any regret for the murder he has committed, replies, "What I felt was less regret than a vague boredom."[6]

There are some helpful insights in a psychoanalytic understanding of boredom that suggest that the superego (the analytical equivalent of conscience), which is conditioned by parents and society, contains and controls the violent and sexual impulses of the id. Think of the superego as the shoulds and oughts and the id as the wants and desires of life. The ego, caught between the two, experiences anxiety as the impulses of the id threaten to break loose and take control. The superego regains control by repression. The ego experiences this as tension, emptiness and a desire for something more—a stimulus hunger. Greenson believes that "this state of affairs . . . is characteristic for all boredom."[7] Haskell Bernstein, another psychoanalyst, says the same thing in a slightly different way:

> The superego . . . has for many grown so restrictive of the experience of intensity that it creates the chronic boredom that afflicts them. . . . The superego's repressing barrier spares the individual the uncomfortable experience of anxiety, but . . . it may exert a severe constricting influence upon the individual's capacity to experience intensity. . . . Then he may be spared the discomfort of anxiety but at the price of chronic boredom.[8]

ALMOST BORED TO DEATH

John Maltsberger, a psychiatrist at Harvard Medical School, describes the remarkable case of Mansur Zasker, "a man almost bored to death." Zasker, who had immigrated to the United States from Pakistan at the age of four, was a thirty-year-old unmarried university graduate. He had recently made a serious suicide attempt. He had made one other attempt ten years earlier. After being seen by various therapists, he was not thought to be clinically depressed. He described his state of mind:

> Most of all I feel extremely bored. Bored of everything—work, friends, hobbies, relationships, music, reading, movies, bored all the time. I do things [merely] to occupy my time, to distract myself from trying to discover the meaning of my existence and I would gladly cease to do anything if the opportunity arose. No matter what the activity is it leaves me feeling unfulfilled. I'm

bored of thinking, of talking, of feeling, bored with being bored. What possible difference does it ultimately make what I do? What difference does anything make? What does it even mean to make a difference? Who cares? . . .

As a child I remember a sense of wonder, a desire to figure out what the world is really all about. Although that wonderment is long gone I'm still preoccupied with the ultimate nature of reality, but resigned to never attaining such awareness.[9]

There is just about enough information here to let us speculate on the reasons for Zasker's extreme and unusual boredom. Several psychotherapists commented on this case. One suggested that his problem was existential despair, not mental illness. Zasker is unable to find meaning in his own life or anywhere in the cosmos. Another therapist suggested that his condition was due to his experience of abandonment, aloneness and anxiety in childhood, when his immigrant parents were working long hours and he himself felt out of place in a new culture: "In the grips of aloneness, the patient is convinced he will be forever cut off from the possibility of human connectedness." Maltsberger, in his concluding comments about this unusual case, reflects more widely on such suicidal tendencies in young people. He quotes an article in the *American Journal of Psychotherapy* titled "Growing Up Dead: Student Suicide," where the author, Herbert Hendin, writes:

Many American families are so filled with tension and rage, so unable to happily adjust to children, that to survive in them at all, parents and children deaden themselves. . . . Too many children are growing up feeling that their mothers and fathers did not regard them as sources of pleasure. Young people today with diminished capacity for enjoyment, or diminished sense of their own ability to give pleasure have for the most part grown up feeling they give little to their parents. Even in cases where the parents did the right thing, the sense of joyless duty was often communicated.[10]

It is probable that all of these factors contributed to Zasker's chronic boredom.

COPING WITH ANXIETY

We have seen how the ego gains relief from anxiety and other uncomfortable or forbidden feelings at the cost of restricting the intensity of feeling and achieving chronic boredom. However, not all psychoanalysts see bore-dom as a defense against deeper anxieties. Some, like Otto Fenichel, admit that more ordinary reasons for boredom exist and contrast "normal" or "in-nocent" boredom with "pathological" boredom.[11] It is only the latter that arises from repressed anxieties.

For example, if people feel inadequate and incompetent at a task, they may experience the resulting anxiety as boredom—a feeling of restlessness and a desire to escape—thus shifting the focus off their interior inadequacy and onto something outside themselves. They can blame an external issue for creating the problem, thus maintaining a more positive self-image and safeguarding self-esteem. Early in medical school I had a hard time under-standing biochemistry. I reacted, to cover my inadequacy, by proclaiming that biochemistry was boring and that was why I got a low grade. I was say-ing to myself, even subconsciously, *I am afraid to commit myself to this. I am going to avoid any chance of vulnerability or failure. Therefore I will not get too involved or care too much about this situation.* Research has demonstrated an association between procrastination and a tendency to boredom. Procrasti-nation is a way of putting off the risk of failure.

An attitude of boredom can also sometimes be a defense mechanism, a response out of our own fear of intimacy and of involvement in relation-ships—again, a fear of failure. Rather than honestly admitting difficulties in relating deeply, Mark maintained a rather distant and arrogant attitude in his relationships with women, maintaining that he had not yet met one who was intellectually compatible. June, who had been sexually abused as a child, kept a safe distance from any physical intimacy with men by claiming that all men were boring chauvinists. In such situations a mask of superior-ity and arrogance may hide a fearful, defensive and wounded spirit. On the outside the person may appear calm and confident.

Arrogance and defensiveness may also arise from a rigid and critical view of the world.[12] This is a particular problem for perfectionists and people who are obsessive—those who believe that they know just how things should be done. When circumstances conspire to threaten this point of view, they may, out of fear or pride, be reluctant to explore unfamiliar situations and activities or to reflect on their own perspective. They may experience their inability or refusal to get engaged as profound boredom and detachment.

Peter McWilliams and John-Roger explore this realm at the boundary of unconscious and conscious experience:

> Boredom is a subtle form of negative thinking that can encompass both anger and fear. Stewart Emery defined boredom as "Hostility without enthusiasm." Fritz Perls called it "The step just before terror." There's a dulling quality about boredom, as though we were numbing something we didn't want to look at. We find people often experience boredom just before they take a step they don't want to take but know they must take. It's usually a step of growth, of movement into their own magnificence. But the step may have fear ("I'm going into uncharted territory") or anger ("Why do I have to do this?"), or both, attached.[13]

A related form of boredom may arise when we make a decision that we later regret. One study of three men and three women ranging in age from sixteen to sixty-seven years old found that they gradually became bored after they had compromised their life projects for less-desired goals. They felt emotionally ambivalent because they were angry with themselves and with others involved in the compromise. They tended to adopt a passive, avoidant attitude and allowed boredom to spread to other aspects of their lives. Disappointed and frustrated, they partially shut down their involvement with the world around them.[14]

As Christians, we know we need some self-protection in this fallen world, but too often we shut down our desires and feelings too much in response to an overload of unpleasant and threatening experiences. Since the Fall, we have been subject to the frustration of our longings. Things rarely work out as we hoped they would. Life is no longer the way it was supposed to be. We harbor feelings of hurt, disappointment, rejection and anger with God. When faced with loss and failure, we find it less painful to deny reality and live with the numbness.

Theologian Henri Nouwen says:

> Our great temptations are boredom and bitterness. When good plans are interrupted by poor weather, our peace of mind by inner turmoil, our hope for peace by a new war, our desire for a stable government by a constant chang-

ing of the guards, and our desire for immortality by real death, we are tempted to give in to paralyzing boredom or to strike back in destructive bitterness.[15]

If we hide these thoughts and feelings from God, and even if we do not honestly admit them to ourselves, we may find that the sense of life and vitality in our relationship with God and with other people begins to ebb away. We may no longer find reading the Bible, prayer or worship interesting or appealing. A cloud of boredom descends on us as we try to protect ourselves and to cut off "inappropriate" feelings toward God—feelings that seem so bad we do not want to admit them to ourselves.

Boredom, once recognized as such, can be a welcome sign. We can welcome it because it should, ideally, prompt us to stop and reflect on the true reason for our boredom and then take appropriate action. We can learn and grow from the experience. Some therapists even encourage people to enter the experience of boredom, to stop numbing and distracting themselves and to allow themselves to feel boredom deeply. As we face it and get to know it more intimately, we can see its roots in and ramifications for our own lives. A friend of mine, who had for many years been in a difficult and distant marriage, was encouraged by her therapist to spend time on a retreat to enter, acknowledge and explore the boredom of her relationship with her husband. She had never thought of her feelings as boredom and was shocked at first by the therapist's suggestion. Later she realized how true this was to her experience. It enabled her to face reality. Intentionally allowing yourself to feel bored may be helpful

> because it gives one the chance to connect with one's soul that boredom had paralyzed. By getting in touch with one's innermost feelings, a new sense of awe is discovered and a new sensitivity is experienced. This usually leads to an enriched life in which the spiritual aspect of being human is recovered. Life moves from black and white to colors; from purely rational to emotive; from coldly calculated to gladly risked; from predictable to adventuresome.[16]

The psalms are wonderful examples of appropriate emotional expressions. King David seems to be deeply aware of his feelings and how they relate to his thoughts. As we read the psalms, it is as if we are listening in on David's many sessions of divine psychoanalysis. David pours out his fears, anger, depression, guilt, shame, grief, thankfulness, joy, delight and worship in the presence of his heavenly Father. Nothing is held back. He has such confidence in God's acceptance that he is able to be utterly honest. He is more fully alive, more passionate in his love for God and hatred of evil. He is acutely aware of the wonders of the natural world, of the glory of the image of God in humankind, and of the pain and brokenness of evil and sin. He shows us how learning to be honest about our inner world is indeed healthy. It is the opposite of shutting down and repressing uncomfortable thoughts and feelings, and it is a great antidote to dryness and boredom.

Throughout the centuries Christians have written about their experiences of apathy and of losing interest in the things of God. As I explored the recorded experiences of the early church fathers and the medieval monks, I found that their accounts resonate strongly with many contemporary descriptions of boredom. I also found helpful clues to distinguish between boredom, depression and the apathy of grief.

8

A TRIP BACK IN TIME
Medieval Boredom, Melancholy and Grief

IF ANY CHAPTER OF THIS BOOK IS TO BE USED as bedtime reading to help you get to sleep, this could be it! You may have to work a bit harder to stay awake, but bear with me. Perhaps it would be best if you read this chapter in the morning, when your brain is more alert and the "yawn count" is lower. However, some of you may love history enough to enjoy tracing the concept of boredom back through the centuries. For you this chapter may be like a cup of coffee: a stimulant that will set your mind going for a few hours. Those who want to skip most of the medieval history should go to the "Depression and Grief" section of this chapter.

We must make an important and practical distinction between boredom, depression and the numbness of grief. But before we do that, let's examine how people in the Middle Ages described their experiences of boredom. Comparing contemporary culture to the cultures in previous centuries will, I hope, throw some light on the phenomenon of boredom. It is important to remember that prior to the eighteenth century, most people in Europe and America believed in God and accepted a Christian view of reality. Hence everything in life was related to spirituality and Christianity. This is hard for us to imagine.

ACEDIA OR SLOTH

The desert fathers were monks who, in the fourth century A.D., retreated from the world to a life of simplicity, contemplation and prayer in order to cultivate their spiritual lives away from the temptations of civilization—money, sex and power. Their modest environment was almost the exact opposite of our overloaded sensory environment. But even there they claimed to experience the visitations of what they called the "noonday demon" who caused them to be bored and dissatisfied with everything in their lives. Evagrius warned his brothers of the need to do battle with this "demon" using the weapons of spiritual disciplines and physical exercise.[1] Was this a real demon, or was it a psychological or physiological phenomenon for which they had no concept?

Many of us experience a noonday slump: a curtain seems to come down over the brain as lunch takes its effect on blood-sugar levels and the biological rhythm slows for a while. The monks, however, were talking about something more; they were addressing a spiritual disorder. This state of mind came to be known in Greek as *akedeia* and in Latin as *acedia*, which means an absence of *kedos* (care), or indifference.[2] The monks lost interest in and passion for the very thing that previously motivated their choices and lifestyle: the pursuit of God and a holy life. Later the word *sloth* was used to describe essentially the same experience, but Gregory the Great and Thomas Aquinas saw "laziness and idleness" (sloth) as one of the "daughters" of *acedia* rather than as the same thing.[3] Some historians separate *acedia* and sloth in this way; others, as we will see, make no clear distinction between them.

Included in the list of the church fathers' seven deadly sins is *acedia*. Some believed it to be the most deadly sin of all because it represented intellectual and spiritual indifference and lethargy. It was a sin, Professor Michael Raposa tells us, caused by "an individual's failure to engage, with vigor and consistency, in appropriate spiritual exercises." And the condition persists because the individual does nothing to alleviate it. Aquinas saw *acedia* as the "opposite of taking joy in the divine good." Raposa sees an example of acedia in the drowsiness of Jesus' disciples in the garden of Gethsemane (Mt 26:36-46) or in the lukewarmness of the church in Laodicea, neither hot nor cold in their devotion to Christ (Rev 3:15-16). Raposa notes that the ancient Israelites were constantly being reminded to avoid "apathy, a hardness of heart resulting in spiritual deafness and blindness, an inability to perceive the word of God" (Is 42:18-19).[4] There is very practical Jewish advice about the danger of sloth in the book of Proverbs. The lazy person is advised, "Go to the ant, you sluggard, consider its ways and be wise" (Prov 6:6). The good wife is praised for not being lazy (Prov 31:10-31).

Dante saw *acedia* as "lukewarmness in well-doing" and "defective love."[5] *Sloth* is defined as "disinclination to action or labor: sluggishness, . . . idleness, indolence" and as "spiritual sluggishness and dejection; apathy and inactivity in the practice of virtue."[6] According to its common meaning in the fourteenth century, *sloth* had come to mean laziness, first in the service of God and then in all other activities. According to its (classical) theological definition from earlier centuries, both *acedia* and sloth described indifference toward and boredom with goodness and God. In *The Canterbury Tales* Geoffrey Chaucer has the parson elaborate on this state of mind in a sermon on the seven deadly sins. "Accidie" (or sloth) is among them, and it makes one "heavy, thoughtful and fretful." The person in the grip of this sin "does all tasks with vexation, slackly and without joy, and is encumbered by doing good. [Accidie] restrains one from prayer. . . . It leads to despair."[7] In *A Catalogue of Sins* William May says:

> Far more serious . . . is the condition of the man who is melancholic and dejected in the very presence of the good. Such a man has his son, but his son bores him. He possesses his beloved, but finds her incapable of stirring his interest. He has been promised the presence of God, but this promise leaves him cold. To such a man the presence or absence of the good makes no difference. His desire for the good is dead. . . . Perhaps boredom is the best modern term to characterize this deadness of soul.[8]

Many theology students have a similar experience. Learning about God all day can leave them feeling weary and bored. Their preoccupation with understanding and analyzing the things of God is not bad in itself, but it should not be mistaken for a real relationship with God. Theologian B. B. Warfield wrote this to such students:

The very atmosphere of your life is these things; you breathe them in at every pore, they surround you, encompass you, press in upon you from every side. It is all in danger of becoming common to you! God forgive you, you are in danger of becoming weary of God![9]

DEADNESS OF SOUL

Acedia was regarded by many of the hermits as the chief of all vices, from which many other sins would flow. He who suffered from it was overcome with weariness, dejection, dislike of everything and everybody around him, laziness and a sense of time passing very slowly; as a result, he usually made various attempts to distract himself or escape into sleep. Feeling indifferent to God, people and the world around him, he found little point to life.[10]

Aquinas examined the spiritual aspect of *acedia* in great detail and used another phrase, which literally means "unhappiness in spiritual good." Seán Healy writes that Aquinas "saw the essence of the sin as *tristitia de spirituali bono,* man's complete lack of interest in, and rejection of, his spiritual good, which, since that is God himself, entails a radical rejection of being itself, one's own and everything else's."[11] He saw it as a choice, whether subconscious or conscious, to turn away from involvement with God and his world. Aquinas, Evagrius and John Cassian all agreed that *acedia* should be dealt with by resistance and persistence. Raposa comments:

One afflicted with this spiritual sorrow is encouraged to persevere in prayer and meditation, precisely because "the more we think about spiritual goods, the more pleasing they become to us." Since the divine good is infinitely pleasing in itself, it offers the best hope of a cure for this disorder. Besieged by boredom and distraction, the mind should hold fast to the object of its contemplation, its loving gaze sustained by a confidence that joy and peace must eventually be restored.[12]

However, some monks, recognizing that much of the work they did from day to day involved repetition, demonstrated more patience and tolerance with this sin than with others. They recognized how hard it is for someone to concentrate for long on one task.

Between the eleventh and twelfth centuries the description of *acedia* and sloth shifted from emphasizing idleness or laziness to suggesting a state of "spiritual slackness, weariness and boredom with religious exercises, lack of fervor, and a state of depression in the ups and downs of spiritual life."[13] From 1200 to 1450 the seven deadly sins were widely known, and the clergy used manuals and catechismal handbooks to teach about and hear confession of spiritual idleness and neglect in performing religious duties. Thus the pastor-confessor had a very important role as "physician of the soul."

DEPRESSION OR LAZINESS?

Two strands of *acedia* emerge in the literature of this period: an emphasis on "sorrow-dejection-despair" and an emphasis on "neglect-idleness-indolence."[14] The former is linked with *tristitia,* which later became melancholia, or what we call depression. Raposa comments that the Renaissance literature on melancholy saw it more as "a disease to be cured than as a sin to be resisted."[15] Franciscan monk David of Augsburg, writing in the thirteenth century, takes this further: he distinguishes three different kinds of the vice of *acedia,* or sloth.[16] Today we would probably distinguish these as, first, clinical depression; second, laziness; and third, spiritual depression or spiritual boredom, which is closest to the early descriptions of sloth and *acedia*—an indifference toward God and his world.

Ignatius of Loyola and John of the Cross also enumerated three causes for this spiritual boredom. The first was sin and the neglect of prayer and other spiritual disciplines. The second (and third for Ignatius) was a time of darkness or desolation sent by God to discipline or test the believer and thus lead him to greater holiness. John combined the discipline and testing into one and thought that a third cause might be "some bad humor or bodily disposition," an organic, physical cause.[17] Note that both of these men saw boredom as both a negative and a positive thing, depending on the cause and the result.

By the sixteenth century, *acedia* was hardly used because the term *melancholy* was preferred for the depressive aspect, while *sloth* became the word to describe neglect, idleness and laziness. The word *acedia* faded from the English language, and by 1621 Robert Burton, writing his huge tome *The Anatomy of Melancholy,* makes only one reference to this state of mind as *taedium vitae* (literally, "boredom with life"). This is a state of mind, comments Healy, of "apparently *inexplicable* boredom, of irrational and unaccountable disgust with life in toto."[18]

Throughout recorded history there is evidence that people of all religions had times of feeling distant from and indifferent about God and their spiritual responsibilities. The causes and effects vary from person to person and often come to light as some sort of spiritual crisis or "dark night of the soul."

One might think that the outward manifestation of sloth or *acedia*—indifference and boredom—might be a retreat into laziness or apathy; but paradoxically, sometimes the very opposite happens: the person becomes very busy and overactive! In fact, Robertson Davies says:

> To be guilty of Acedia it is not necessary to be physically sluggish at all. You can be as busy as a bee. You can fill your days with activity, bustling from meeting to meeting, sitting on committees, running from one party to another in a perfect whirlwind of movement. But if, meanwhile, your feelings and sensibilities are withering, if your relationships with people near to you are becoming more and more superficial, if you are losing touch even with yourself, it is Acedia which has claimed you for its own.[19]

It is the sense of having lost feeling for God, people, the world and oneself that is so characteristic of severe *acedia* and that is so closely related to the contemporary experience of serious boredom. Os Guinness describes sloth as "inner despair at the worthwhileness of the worthwhile that finally slumps into an attitude of 'Who cares?' "[20] Some might say, "Whatever!"

I was fascinated to find that in the scientific and religious literature of the sixteenth century, the debate over responsibility for one's feelings and thoughts was almost as lively as it has been in the twentieth. At the heart of the debate are these questions: Am I completely responsible for my boredom? What do I do to respond to it? Are depression and apathy about life a result of temperament, sin, sickness or all three? Does the person need sympathy and a hug, a challenge and a kick, medication, or perhaps all of the above to get him or her going?

On the side of personal responsibility, T. H. Wright suggests that this "fatal surrender of initiative is not the result of any trying ordeal of life, which in a measure might excuse it, but is just the formation of a desperately bad habit. The 'malady of not wanting' is a serious ailment of life in all its stages."[21] One of the features that characterize the writings about sloth and *acedia* is that, apart from some exceptions, they are seen as sins for which the person is responsible! Loss of appetite and passion for life, deadness of soul, boredom with good and God all sound like a malignant disease of the person's inner being. Could this be just a "desperately bad habit"? Certainly some people are lazy and have a hard time feeling strongly about anything in life. Rather than seeing it as simply either a bad habit or a disease, we may more accurately see it as a complex formula, as the end result of a combination of a particular temperament, a lack of self-discipline and certain values and beliefs about life.

DEPRESSION AND GRIEF

One very important and practical distinction that must be carefully clarified is the difference between the state of mind of *acedia* and sloth, on the one hand, and two closely related experiences, clinical depression and the numbness and sorrow of bereavement, on the other. Both boredom and depression "involve the horror of experienced helplessness."[22] William Cowper, a great eighteenth-century poet and hymn writer who suffered from intermittent serious depression, gives us insight into this condition. He wrote:

> You describe delightful scenes, but you describe them to one who, if he even saw them, could receive no delight from them; who has a faint recollection, and so faint as to be like an almost forgotten dream, that once he was susceptible of pleasure from such causes. . . . Why is scenery like this, I had almost said, why is the very scene which many years since I could not contemplate without rapture, now become, at the best, an insipid wilderness?[23]

This sounds very much like the experience of *acedia* or boredom, but other signs and symptoms of clinical depression are present which enable us to distinguish this state of apathy about the world from ordinary boredom. If I was concerned that someone was depressed, I would ask about his or her appetite (too much or too little), sleep disturbances (difficulty falling asleep, waking too early), and problems with concentration, sadness, suicidal thoughts and tearfulness (occurring every day for at least two consecutive weeks). Unlike the bored person, the depressed person has a very negative view of herself. She usually feels a great sense of inadequacy and self-blame, together with a lack of desire to do anything. She may sit for hours in the same chair; she may avoid company; and she may lose all interest in work, food and sex. The very bored person is usually deeply dissatisfied with the world around him, but he still feels desire and wants to do something, though he does not know what to do. Symptoms of depression in teenagers and ad-olescents are likely to vary from these accepted diagnostic criteria with non-specific symptoms such as boredom, anxiety, academic failure, relationship difficulties and sleep disturbance predominating.[24] Depressed adolescents, in an exaggeration of their normal sleep pattern, will usually sleep a long time and be very reluctant to get up and face another difficult day. Adults will more typically suffer from early morning waking and disturbed sleep.

It is vital to recognize clinical depression because such a diagnosis de-mands a full physical examination by a doctor to rule out any physical cause, and the patient will almost certainly require counseling or psychotherapy and antidepressants combined.

Andrew Solomon, a writer, described his experience as he began to slip into what proved to be a very serious bout of depression:

> In June 1994, I began to be constantly bored. My first novel had recently been published in England, and yet its favorable reception did little for me. I read the reviews indifferently and felt tired all the time. In July, back home in downtown New York, I found myself burdened by phone calls, social events, conversation. The subway proved intolerable. In August, I started to feel numb. I didn't care about work, family, or friends. My writing slowed, then stopped. My usually headstrong libido evaporated. All this made me feel that I was losing my self. Scared, I tried to schedule pleasures. I went to parties and failed to have fun, saw friends and failed to connect; I bought things I had previously wanted and gained no satisfaction from them.[25]

J. M. Barbalet also wrestles with the distinction between boredom and de-pression. Boredom is a "restless feeling of dissatisfaction" with an absence of in-terest in activity and circumstance, whereas depression is usually characterized by "despondency . . . fatigue and resignation."[26] The depressed person tends to blame himself; the bored person tends to be irritated with the circumstances.

The experience of grief is similar to boredom—little interest in what once gave great joy. Hamlet says it well:

> I have of late—but
> wherefore I know not—lost all my mirth, forgone all
> custom of exercises; and indeed it goes so heavily
> with my disposition that this goodly frame, the
> earth, seems to me a sterile promontory.[27]

Recently a client told me that since the death of a good friend eight months previous, she had lost all interest in her usual much-loved pursuits of reading, listening to music, photography and walking in nature. The world had turned from color to black and white or monochrome gray.

Grief normally passes with time (a few months to two years) and with talking to family and friends, but sometimes the process gets stuck and the grieving person needs professional help. Depression or grief may cause a sense of apathy, boredom and indifference to life. But sometimes it works the opposite way, and boredom is one of the many causes of depression. One can think of boredom, depression and grief as three overlapping circles.

There is certainly considerable common ground between the experiences of our ancestors—which they called *acedia*, sloth, *tristitia*, *taedium vitae* and melancholy—and our contemporary experiences of boredom, depression and grief! It is important to recognize certain differences so that appropriate help may be offered.

It is obvious from this historical excursion that the experience of boredom is not unique to our culture or generation. In the next chapter, before we return to the twenty-first century, our journey through time will take us into the eighteenth century and beyond, a time when many Europeans and Americans were abandoning the previously widespread Christian understanding of life and culture. Here we may find some more clues in our search for the causes of boredom.

9

FROM SIN TO SELF-FULFILLMENT

Religion, the Right to Happiness
and Lack of Inner Resources

WE HAVE ALREADY DISCUSSED CHRISTIANITY'S profound influence on early European culture. Prior to the nineteenth century most people would accept personal responsibility for their own feelings and usually believed that boredom was a sin or the result of some inner deficiency. In both Europe and America, there was a general acceptance of a Christian view of God and life. People did not expect a quick fix to their problems or a pill for every ill. They were more prepared to sacrifice their own self-satisfaction in order to help others, and they usually expected that life would be difficult and often tedious. They had a higher motive for enduring unhappiness and struggle when it came, believing that life in the hereafter would be so much better. Not only did they have a hope for the future, they also had a reason for living in the present, however difficult it was. They had a reason, too, to be thankful in seasons when they were happy and life was enjoyable. Contentment was preached as an important virtue. People felt responsible to work hard and to take an interest in and be involved with life, especially regarding their family and wider social responsibilities. They saw boredom as a sign of weakness, sin or a lack of moral fiber. The ordinary things of life should be, they believed, seen as gifts of God and, as such, enough to satisfy and keep a person from being bored. One who sought extra pleasure was seen as someone to be pitied, even scorned.

This was expressed forcefully in the language of a 1765 sermon by James Fordyce:

> There is not, methinks, any thing more contemptible, or more to be pitied, than that turn of mind, which finding no entertainment in itself, none at home, none in books, none in rational conversation, nor in the intercourses of real friendship, nor in ingenious works of any kind, is continually seeking to stifle reflection in a tumult of pleasures, and to divert weariness in a crowd.[1]

Samuel Butler does not mince his words: "The man who lets himself be bored is even more contemptible than the bore."[2]

SHRIVELING OF INNER RESOURCES

Although the bored person's inner weakness was usually seen as a sin, it was also sometimes considered to be due to a shriveling of inner resources. This idea comes through strongly in one of John Berryman's poems:

> Life, friends, is boring. We must not say so.
> After all, the sky flashes, the great sea yearns,
> we ourselves flash and yearn,
> and moreover my mother told me as a boy
> (repeatingly) "Ever to confess you're bored
> means you have no
> Inner Resources." I conclude now I have no
> inner resources, because I am heavy bored.
>
> Peoples bore me,
> literature bores me, especially great literature,
> Henry bores me, with his plights & gripes
> as bad as achilles,
> who loves people and valiant art, which bores me.[3]

The implication of Berryman's poem is that it is a failure of character to have no inner resources to enjoy the wonders of creation, literature and people. Such abilities and resources should be cultivated and developed early in life. We could use our imaginations to relieve boredom by finding some inner stimulation.[4] But if there is lack of development or shriveling on the inside, perhaps more and more stimulation is needed from the outside in order for one to feel alive. And as if the labels "interior inadequacy," "shriveled resources" and "sin" were not enough, an essay in 1780 portrayed victims of boredom as suffering from "diseased imagination."[5]

Some people seem to be gifted from an early age with great sensitivity, curiosity, imagination and creativity, and hence they rarely experience boredom. At the opposite end of the spectrum are people who seem to have little of these resources. I have occasionally met people who seem so disinterested and unengaged with life that they remind me of those T. S. Eliot described as "hollow" or "empty." As with other gifts—such as intelligence and physical strength—imagination, creativity and interest in life are innate parts of how we are created. But these gifts can either be cultivated, strengthened and developed or ignored, suppressed and allowed to wither and even die. Some aspects of our culture strengthen these inner resources and other aspects suppress their development.

I find that when a piece of music on the radio or a newspaper article fails to immediately grab my interest, I will often change channels or move on to something else. It takes a certain discipline of mind to put effort into getting past the initial reaction of disinterest and pursuing something further until interest is sparked. When we meet someone we find boring, it is hard to maintain a curiosity that wants to discover who is behind the façade, even though we know that few people are really boring once we get to know them well. Emily Post, writing on etiquette in the 1940s (with a flavor of eighteenth-century moralism), criticizes people who are boring, but says:

> On the other hand, to be bored is a bad habit, and one only too easy to fall into. As a matter of fact, it is impossible, almost, to meet anyone who has not *something* of interest to tell you if you are but clever enough yourself to find out what it is. Also you might remember that in every conversation with a "dull" person, half of the dullness is your own. There are certain delightful people who refuse to be bored. . . . If you find yourself sitting in the hedgerow with nothing but weeds, there is no reason for shutting your eyes and seeing nothing, instead of finding what beauty you may in the weeds.[6]

There is truth in this perspective: we need to keep our imaginations alive and learn to exercise the proactive muscles of involvement in the world lest we become flabby and weak and boring and bored. This idea that boredom arises from sinful or weak passivity stands in stark contrast to the common contemporary attitude of seeking, almost demanding, that our needs for entertainment and excitement be met—not by our own effort so much as by the flick of a switch, the press of a button on the remote control or the click of a mouse. Perhaps a link exists between the increase of narcissism and self-centeredness that many psychiatrists have noticed in the last century and the concurrent increase in boredom.

THE DECLINE OF RELIGION

In the post-Enlightenment atmosphere of the eighteenth and nineteenth centuries, people in Europe and North America began to turn away from the pursuit of God, where happiness was a byproduct rather than an end in itself, and toward the pursuits of happiness and self-fulfillment for their own sake. People threw off what they saw as the shackles and inhibiting restraints of religion. They no longer depended on God because they increasingly believed that science, reason or even aesthetic experience would give them the answers to life's questions. They thought that they could find the meaning and purpose of life without reference to the divine. This culminated in the twentieth century with the Humanist Manifesto, which stated humanity's autonomy most succinctly:

> We find insufficient evidence for belief in the existence of a supernatural; it is either meaningless or irrelevant to the question of the survival and fulfillment of the human race. As non-theists, we begin with humans not God, nature not deity. . . . We can discover no divine purpose or providence for the human species. . . . No deity will save us; we must save ourselves.[7]

A. N. Wilson recently chronicled the history of this abandonment of God in a book titled *God's Funeral*. He borrows this title from the 1908-1910 poem by Thomas Hardy. In the middle of this poem, Hardy mourns the loss of a belief in a comforting presence and hope:

> So, toward our myth's oblivion,
> Darkling, and languid-lipped, we creep and grope,
> Sadlier than those who wept in Babylon

Whose Zion was a still abiding hope.

How sweet it was in years far hied
To start the wheels of day with trustful prayer,
To lie down liegely at the eventide
And feel a blest assurance he was there!
And who or what shall fill his place?
Whither will wanderers turn distracted eyes.

There is a wistful longing for a story that makes sense of life, for a perceived reality that was a basis for trust in something bigger than ourselves but that has now been abandoned as "myth"—a comforting but unnecessary illusion.

THE RIGHT TO HAPPINESS

The "death of God" school of philosophy promoted a view that society, rather than religion, should now provide all we need. The sense of entitlement to happiness increased.[8] The Declaration of Independence's assumption of our right to "life, liberty and the pursuit of happiness" enshrined this idea.

Humanistic and antireligious sentiments affected every discipline but were, until very recently, particularly felt in the fields of sociology and psychology, where truth and happiness would be found through the subjective psychological experience of authenticity. In 1961 psychologist Carl Rogers wrote:

> *Experience is, for me, the highest authority.* . . . It is to experience that I must return again and again, to discover a closer approximation to truth as it is in the process of becoming in me. Neither the Bible nor the prophets—neither Freud nor research—neither the revelations of God nor man—can take precedence over my own direct experience.[9]

From this perspective happiness and the meaning of life come from deep within us, not from anything outside. Nothing is as reliable as my own subjective experience (Rogers and others would argue), and I can pursue self-fulfillment without reference to any higher authority.

Now there is obviously a problem when self-fulfillment becomes the foundational guiding principle in life. Our perception of what meets our needs and makes us feel good will be the primary motivator of our behavior. If we feel bored and dissatisfied in marriage, we might feel justified in leaving our spouse for someone else who can make us happy.

FOCUS ON FEELINGS

Whether we find something fulfilling or boring depends very much on what we expect from it and how the culture around us shapes our expectations and desires. The advertising and entertainment industries are especially eager to persuade us that they can meet our every need, and they may even help us to become aware of needs and desires that we never knew we had! If their techniques for influencing us were not successful, I doubt they would spend millions of dollars for a thirty-second commercial during the Super Bowl or the Academy Awards. My ability to be content with a vacation in a rough cabin by a lake may be compromised if I have been looking at a lot of travel magazines and brochures showing exotic Caribbean beaches. If I am seduced by the alluring online advertisements for exciting pornography, with its false portrayal of sexuality and beauty, I may find it very hard not to be bored by the responsibilities, ordinary routines and commitments of marriage that in reality prepare a foundation for the greatest enjoyment of sex. When my feelings rule me, I am intolerant of pain and boredom; I demand that my needs for pleasure and distraction be met as quickly as possible. Today, when there is no greater principle to guide us, we tend to allow our desires and passions (which are so easily shaped by the culture) to rule us. "Obey your thirst" and "unleash your lust," say the advertisements.

FINDING FAULT—OUT THERE!

The Romantics of the nineteenth and twentieth centuries, in their sensitivity to society and nature and their love for "the ideal of a free and natural life," recognized that boredom was not always the individual's fault. They drew attention to the many aspects of the culture of their time (such as class structure, bureaucracy, factories and machines) that caused emotional repression and hampered freedom of the spirit. "Doing so," writes Orrin Klapp, "they shifted blame for boredom and ennui from the lazy or rebellious individual to society, turning a fault of an individual into a reproach against a social order whose rules are oppressive."[10] Sociologists from the turn of the century, notably Max Weber and Émile Durkheim, have discussed the phenomenon and causes of boredom among the working classes, who are caught like cogs in the machine of routine and bureaucracy and live humdrum lives with little subjective significance. Cut off from the larger decisions of organizations, they become increasingly alienated. Durkheim used the word *anomie,* by which he meant a lack of cohesion and order in society with weak social bonds between people.[11] He believed that it contributed to an increased likelihood of boredom, depression and suicide. Klapp summarizes Durkheim's view:

> Disintegration of social bonds, especially rapid rises of status, remove needed constraints from the individual, opening him to boundless desires and insatiable striving which result not in happiness but boredom. Anomie gives rise to "greed," also "a thirst arises for novelties, unfamiliar pleasures, nameless sensations, all of which lose their savor once known."[12]

Even with this sociological recognition of the external causes of boredom, the person who complains of it is still stigmatized. Admitting and displaying boredom, until recently, has been considered rude and improper, a sign of personal failure. Perhaps the shift in attitude from the eighteenth-century view means that now people who are bored blame their environment rather than themselves. But those around the bored person still often see him or her as inadequate.

Some things are inherently boring because of their repetitiveness, yet some boredom is created in our minds because of our own attitudes. In most cases it is too simplistic to give an either-or answer to the question of responsibility. We must consider each situation in its own right to get some sense of who or what is responsible for the boredom and what can be done to relieve it. We have seen many influences in our culture and in the individual choices that people make in response to their circumstances that might lead to a "shriveling of inner resources." I am arguing that parts of the entertainment culture are both a cause and an effect of the shriveling of inner resources.

We have begun to trace the relationship that Patricia Spacks suggested between the rise of boredom and three things: the decline of Christianity, the sense of entitlement to happiness and an emphasis on subjective experience or on following my inner desires. In the next chapter we will pursue the cause of existential boredom and this will take us into a struggle with the big questions of life.

10

HAUNTED BY HOPELESSNESS

*Postmodernism, Indifference
and the Loss of Meaning*

BEHIND THE BRIGHT LIGHTS, BUSYNESS and outward optimism of our culture lurk some haunting questions that many people want to ignore. Perhaps they can recall a time in their idealistic youth when they asked these questions but found no satisfying answers. Why am I here on this planet? Who am I? Can I know anything with certainty? What is the purpose of life? Why get up in the morning? These "heavy" topics tend to be conversation killers in most situations. It is more acceptable to talk about sports, sex, relationships, work and the latest soap opera, television show or movie. Of course, some movies can be profoundly disturbing because behind the entertainment they sometimes ask the "big questions." The amazingly popular movie *The Matrix* (which many young people saw at least five or six times) invites reflection on the purpose of our existence.[1] It makes frequent use of religious (mostly Christian) symbolism, and viewers are confronted with the ultimate question of whether there is anything worth dying for in this strange reality where we are often tempted to escape into fantasy and virtual reality. The main characters in the disturbing film *American Beauty* are trying to find some meaning and beauty in their ordinary lives. Lester is looking for something more. He says "I have lost something. . . . I'm not sure what. . . . I feel so sedated." His wife is consumed with searching for happiness in her perfect garden, perfect clothes, furniture, meals and sexual fantasies.[2] The less well-known movie *Run Lola Run* opens with the narrator asking, "Who are we? Where do we come from? Where are we going? How do we know what we think we know? Why do we believe anything at all? Countless questions in search of an answer."[3] In this love story, three alternative fragmented, post-modern versions of a particular event force the viewer to reflect on the significance of relationships and the meaning of life and death.

Looking back over the history of culture and philosophy we can see that modernism—the faith that reason, science, psychology, art or something in this world will save us—has, in many people's eyes, failed. Most people no longer think that they need to be "saved" from or by anyone or anything. Since the Enlightenment we have discovered that we are nothing more than complex animals or machines in the grip of an evolutionary process. We began by chance; we will end by chance. The idealism of previous generations has turned to cynicism and lack of hope. This mood has spread to many parts of our world, especially those devastated by war, famine, AIDS and other disasters. It is also found behind the glamour and glitz of the lives of the rich and famous.

Many have come to believe that there are no answers to the big questions of life, and some even believe there are no meaningful questions! They believe that there is certainly no one truth that is normative for everyone—except of course the truth that there is no one truth normative for everyone! They say that we can no longer find meaning in the objective external world. We each find our own subjective reality and truth. All belief systems are equally plausible and true. This perspective on life is often called *postmodernism*. Rather than asking, "Is it true?" or "Did it really happen?" the postmodern person asks, "Who cares?" or perhaps, more pragmatically, "Will it meet my needs?"

The extreme of this is seen in the influential philosophy of Jacques Derrida, often called *deconstructionism*, in which every statement is questioned.[4] The world, in this view, is merely a "construct" of our mind and language. The language of the deconstructionists dances frustratingly around any commitment to opinion or claim to truth or reality.

For some, this subjective and relativistic view is felt as a great freedom to

be whoever they want to be. The challenge for the consistent postmodernist is to create a new and exciting self and reality each day. Theologian
Michael Williams observes: "If the postmodern channel-surfer had not aris-
en, consumerism would have had to invent him. I need to have at least ten
different personas so that I can consume all the goods that materialist culture wants me to consume."[5]

For others who try to live consistently by postmodernism, they know
that this philosophy works while living alone in the world of the Internet or
fantasy but that it is much harder to live this way in real day-to-day relationships. An attempt to live while believing that there is no ultimate
meaning or purpose, that there is no point in even looking for these, can be
very depressing; at the very least, life becomes profoundly boring. Nothing
is of real significance or importance. An example of this is seen in the movie
Reality Bites, where one of the main characters says, "There's no point to
anything. . . . It's all just a random lottery of meaningless tragedy in a series
of near escapes."[6] James Kunen caught this loss of hope and the sense of
powerlessness in some interviews in Greenwich Village. He reported these
in a 1997 *Time* magazine article titled "It Ain't Us Babe!"

> "This is a disgusting generation. It's a disgusting time to live in. It's boring,"
> says Alexandra Lynn, who is 15 going on 25, as she languidly smokes a ciga-
> rette with a gaggle of similarly jaded teens in Greenwich Village's Washington
> Square Park on a sultry Wednesday night. "The '90s is an exhausted decade.
> There's nothing to look for, and nowhere to go. This generation really hasn't
> got any solid ground. I mean, the '60s had solid ground, but that's gone now."
> . . . For those of Alexandra's generation, us-vs.-them causes are hard to find.
> They already *have* peace and freedom, the Holy Grail of the '60s. "But with
> that," she says, "comes the monotonous undertone of the entirety of life, you
> know? What is there to do? There's nothing to do, there's nothing to stand
> for, there's nothing even to look at, because the shock value is gone."
>
>   Her park buddy Harry Siegel, 19, elaborates on this point. "The ability to
> howl at the moon is lost," he laments. "The counterculture has been ab-
> sorbed by the culture. The blue hair and pierced nipples are trite, and no one
> pays them any mind. Nothing is outside the fold . . . " "There's nothing to do
> but entertainment—make it or watch it. The '60s and whatever it stood for
> have mutated into something that's just another show."[7]

This *Time* article was obviously written before the shocking events of September 11, 2001. Now it would be difficult to say the same thing. Even the most ardent relativist and proponent of tolerance has been faced with the reality of something that the majority defines as evil. Most people emerged from their normal humdrum lives, at least for a while, with a new passion for life and an enjoyment of the simple pleasures of day-to-day existence. Most now support the war against terrorism. We often speak of "the day that changed our lives"—a day that shook us out of our cultural indifference and boredom, at least temporarily. Many people today live somewhere in the tension between modernism (a faith in science, a belief that there is some answer somewhere) and postmodernism (cynicism about any claims of universal "truth").

TOLERANCE AND INDIFFERENCE—"WHATEVER"

Prior to September 11, the cultural value of tolerance made it hard to take a stand on anything except the value of tolerance of all beliefs and behavior. A 1990s bumper sticker read, "Who knows? Who cares? Why bother?" I heard one high school student complaining recently that "the more you care about something the more unpopular you are!" It is certainly not cool to feel too much passion about anything, unless you passionately like pop culture or passionately dislike the narrow-mindedness of anyone who believes in truth, goodness or beauty.

Dorothy Sayers, writing long before "tolerance" was so fashionable and politically correct and before it had become the highest value of our culture, makes a rather disturbing connection between tolerance and the medieval Latin word for apathy and boredom, *acedia:*

> In the world it *[acedia]* is called Tolerance, but in hell it is called Despair. . . .
> It is the sin that believes in nothing, cares for nothing, seeks to know nothing, interferes with nothing, enjoys nothing, hates nothing, finds purpose in nothing, lives for nothing, and remains alive because there is nothing for which it will die.[8]

This seems to be a very negative view of tolerance, one that ignores its vital importance in helping to break down racial, ethnic, gender and religious prejudices and hatred. But Sayers is saying that when tolerance becomes the supreme and most important virtue, we cannot express any evaluation of anyone else's actions or beliefs without being labeled as bigoted or prejudiced. When everything is allowed in the name of tolerance, then there is nothing worth standing for, and as a result the soul begins to wither and die. A sense of apathy and a disengagement from life takes over. A feeling that everything is tedious and annoying underlies all thoughts.

Philosopher Peter Kreeft writes:

> Indifference is more fashionable today than it ever was before, except perhaps once: as Rome was dying—decadent, sophisticated, skeptical, relativistic, jaded, bored and promiscuous, skidding down its own mudslide of spiritual waste—exactly like us. By contrast, all young and healthy nations, eras, cultures and individuals are simple, strong and passionate—never bland, indifferent and relativistic. If there is any certain symptom of social senility it is indifference, shown in slogans like "anything goes," "do your own thing," "different strokes for different folks," or "live and let live."[9]

When tolerance becomes the supreme virtue, as it has for many in our Western world, it is politically incorrect to be passionate about anything except tolerance and the equal truth of everyone's point of view. People get surprisingly intolerant whenever they perceive others being intolerant!

The philosopher Friedrich Nietzsche, one of the fathers of existentialism, who had abandoned any belief in one God or any higher purpose, wrote "Against boredom even gods struggle in vain"[10] because there is no bigger story that gives meaning to their day-to-day adventures. One of my students wrote, "While studying existentialism I felt huge sympathy with the views presented: the absurdity and nothingness of our human condition. I started to feel bored with life as a whole, as if nothing I did had any meaning anyway."

I was intrigued to discover that according to the *Oxford English Dictionary*, the early root of the word *interesting,* the opposite of *boring,* is from a Latin verb form meaning "it makes a difference, matters, is of importance." A shift in meaning occurred at the end of the eighteenth century, and the word *interesting* now relates less to objective realities than to a subjective feeling. *Interesting* is now defined as "adapted to excite interest; having the qualities that rouse curiosity, engage attention, or appeal to the emotions."[11]

LOSS OF FAITH AND MEANING

Patricia Spacks, reflecting on the apparent increase in boredom in the last three hundred years, believes that one of the possible reasons for this is the decline of orthodox Christianity.

> As a twentieth-century theologian has pointed out, boredom can usefully be understood as faith's opposite. "Where faith, for good or bad, is a tremendous drive toward relationship and contains all the energies that we associate with the life of wishing and longing, boredom moves in just the opposite way." . . . The history of commentary on boredom . . . shows a steady decline in faith.[12]

Seàn Healy sees the root causes of the increase in what he calls "hyperboredom" as "the growing metaphysical void at the center of Western civilization" and the fading of a "sense of transcendence."[13]

Existentialist writers in the 1920s and 1930s seem to have a keen sense of the significance of the loss of a Judeo-Christian foundation to European culture and the resultant loss of meaning. Martin Heidegger saw boredom as a basic mood and wrote of the fundamental questions of metaphysics: "Why are there essents, rather than nothing? . . . The question is upon us in boredom, when we are equally removed from joy and despair, and everything about us seems so hopelessly commonplace that we no longer care whether anything is or is not." "All things, and we with them sink into a kind of indifference. . . . There is nothing to hold onto."[14] George Bernanos writes of a country priest reflecting on this universal condition, as if it were an invisible plague:

> The world is eaten up by boredom. . . . You can't see it all at once. It is like dust. You go about and never notice. . . . But stand still for an instant and there it is, coating your face and hands. . . . The world has long been familiar with boredom . . . such is the true condition of man. No doubt the seed was scattered all over life, and here and there found fertile soil to take root; but I wonder if man has ever before experienced this contagion, this leprosy of boredom; an aborted despair, a turpid variety of despair that, without a doubt, is like the fermentation of a decomposing Christianity.[15]

Albert Camus, Franz Kafka and Jean Paul Sartre all reflected on the problem of the meaninglessness of life when there is no God to give it meaning. As touched on earlier, Samuel Beckett's plays, especially *Waiting for Godot*, made meaninglessness and boredom the central themes of the drama. Pierre Teilhard de Chardin wrote of boredom as "the underlying cause of all our troubles."[16] Karl Jaspers spoke of the "despiritualization of the world . . . [as] one of the possible consequences of a mental development which here has actually led to Nothingness."[17] Nietzsche wrote:

> The time has come when we have to pay for having been Christians for two thousand years: we are losing the center of gravity by virtue of which we have lived. . . .
>
> The entire idealism of mankind hitherto is on the point of changing suddenly into nihilism, into the belief in absolute *worth*lessness, i.e., *meaning*lessness.[18]

W. B. Yeats picked up this theme in his poem "The Second Coming":

> Things fall apart; the centre cannot hold;
> Mere anarchy is loosed upon the world. . . .
> The best lack all conviction, while the worst
> Are full of passionate intensity.[19]

With the center gone—with a loss of relationship to what Heidegger calls "Being"—there is a profound sense of anxiety and boredom. "All things, and we with them, sink into a sort of indifference," wrote Heidegger. "There is nothing to hold on to."[20] Healy comments that boredom tends to appear in times of "cultural disintegration." Communities and cultures with a strong sense of purpose and direction do not suffer much from this malady. Healy contrasts the Christian Puritan communities, with their high sense of calling, to the "epoch of boredom" of the "latter days of the Roman Empire, a time of relaxed authority and weakened moral imperatives."[21]

The history of philosophy in Europe and North America over the last three hundred years is the story of throwing off the restraints and shackles of Christianity and attempting to find a basis for meaning and significance in science, reason or experience—without reference to God.

Nietzsche, the passionate prophet of such atheism, said, "I come too early. . . . My time is not yet. This tremendous event [the death of God] . . . has not yet reached the ears of men."[22] Healy makes the argument that Nietzsche claimed God "died of boredom." Nietzsche's appeal was to move on beyond the boring "bourgeois religiosity of the pharisaism of his age." He found, says Healy, "the dreariness of the mediocre, shop-soiled, sleazy, utterly worn-out pieties of the nineteenth century intolerable."[23] He announced the "death of God" with enthusiasm and excitement: "We philosophers and 'free spirits' feel, when we hear the news that the 'old god is dead' as if a new dawn shone on us; our heart overflows with gratitude, amazement, premonitions, expectation."[24]

While some recognized that the loss of a Christian framework led to a loss of meaning and, hence, to boredom with life, Nietzsche was excited by the idea of getting rid of what he saw as the bourgeois and boringly repressive influence of Christianity and of thus being able to live with much greater freedom. Sartre, another father of existentialism, commented:

> If I've excluded God the Father, there must be somebody to invent values. . . .
> To say that we invent values means neither more nor less than this; that there is no sense in life *a priori*. . . . It is yours to make sense of, and the value of it is nothing else but the sense that you choose.[25]

Mihaly Csikszentmihalyi has spent more than thirty years researching the nature of happiness and satisfaction with life. His popular book *Flow: The Psychology of Optimal Experience* ends with the chapter "The Making of Meaning." To avoid boredom we need to have a sense of meaning and purpose in life. He acknowledges that many people have found this in religious belief. "Such implicit faith used to be widespread in our culture . . . but it is not easy to find it now. Many of us have to discover a goal that will give meaning to life on our own, without the help of a traditional faith."[26] An areligious person cannot rely on anything but science.

> There is no one *out there* to tell us, "Here is a goal worth spending your life on." Because there is no absolute certainty to which to turn, each person must discover ultimate purpose on his or her own. . . .
> It is relatively easy to bring order to the mind for short stretches of time; any realistic goal can accomplish this. A good game, an emergency at work, a happy interlude at home will focus attention and produce the harmonious experience of flow. But it is much more difficult to extend this state of being through the entirety of life.[27]

Csikszentmihalyi's own ultimate sense of meaning is found in understanding and cooperating with the process of evolution so that "the problem of meaning will then be resolved as the individual's purpose merges with the universal flow."[28]

Victor Frankl, an Austrian psychiatrist, wrote in *Man's Search for Meaning* about his own experience in the concentration camps of the World War II, where he was interned for several years. The prisoners who had some sense of purpose in life, such as writing a book or escaping, survived the incredible boredom and the intolerable conditions. The others usually got sick and died.[29]

THE SEARCH FOR A FOUNDATION

We have lived with this so-called humanist and existential freedom for a long time now, and references to boredom in the culture have only multiplied. We have seen the many ways in which people try to escape meaninglessness. The writer of the book of Ecclesiastes describes how he tried to find satisfaction in every possible form of activity, work, wealth, pleasure, houses, gardens and many beautiful women. Instead, he ended up with a sense of emptiness that is so often the lot of those who have everything:

> I denied myself nothing my eyes desired;
> I refused my heart no pleasure.
> My heart took delight in all my work,
> and this was the reward for all my labor.
> Yet when I surveyed all that my hands had done
> and what I had toiled to achieve,
> everything was meaningless, a chasing after the wind;
> nothing was gained under the sun. (Eccles 2:10-11)

In the late 1980s many Silicon Valley high-tech millionaires achieved their dreams and were able to retire at an early age. John McLaren, writing in the London *Sunday Times*, observed their common fate:

> They all went down the same path. They acquired vast houses in swanky neighborhoods, Ferraris and Mercs, cute personal trainers, serious golf coaches, and copies of Luxury Hotels of the World. For me it was like watching a

very ornate clock run down. Around 15 months later, with no more toys left to buy, they stared out over their manicured lawns and realized to their horror that they were bored out of their skulls. And that another 40 years of this lay ahead.[30]

When I first gave a lecture on boredom, someone told me of a friend who had worked on the development of the Lockheed F22 plane for fifteen years of his working life. The great day came when the plane first flew, and after all the excitement he turned to his wife and said, "Is that all?" Our work does give us some satisfaction and purpose for a while because God intended it that way. However, without a sense of ultimate meaning or purpose, without a story (or metanarrative) that makes sense of our individual story, without a connection to the deeper reality of how we are made, that temporary work will not be enough.

We are not made to find meaning in the things that can be experienced with the five senses. Living as if our sole purpose could be found in this way is like a fish trying to live on land or a bird trying to live under water. Augustine's famous saying puts it simply and well: "Thou hast formed us for Thyself and our hearts are restless till they find rest in Thee."[31] In our frenetic age we run after any diversion in an attempt to avoid introspection and awareness of our incompleteness and dissatisfaction. Pascal wrote, "The sole cause of man's unhappiness is that he does not know how to stay quietly in his room." He knew that when a person is alone and without distractions, it is hard to suppress the big questions that begin to move into one's consciousness. "In busyness," Pascal continues, "we have a narcotic to keep us from brooding and take our mind off these things."[32] "These things" are, of course, the ultimate questions about the nature and meaning of existence. Theologian and philosopher Jacques Ellul wrote that "people today are victims of emptiness—devoid of meaning. Busy, but emotionally empty, open to all entreaties and in search of something to fill the inner void. For this we go to popular entertainment."[33]

Walker Percy, whose novels are often populated with bored people, explores this theme in *Lost in the Cosmos: The Last Self-Help Book.* In a section titled "Why the Self Is the Only Object in the Cosmos Which Gets Bored," Percy questions why the word *boredom* did not enter the language until the eighteenth century. He wonders whether the word *bore* may have come from the French verb *bourrer*, which means "to stuff," and asks:

> Is it because there is a special sense in which for the past two or three hundred years the self has perceived itself as a left over which cannot be accounted for by its own objective view of the world and that in spite of an ever heightened self-consciousness, increased leisure, ever more access to cultural and recreational facilities, ever more instruction on self-help, self-growth, self-enrichment, the self feels ever more imprisoned in itself[?] . . . Boredom is the self stuffed with the self. [34]

With no outside reference point to give value to the self, we are left only with finding meaning and identity in our work, our lifestyle or in one intense experience after another—these give us a sense of being alive and important. The world around us becomes a series of mirrors in which we find ourselves. Andrew Fellows observes:

> We run from one to the next in this flimsy system, like ghosts trapped in an existential vacuum. How can a ghost feel alive and real? The answer is intense experience. In a world where the reality of things no longer gives life to the self, intense experience is all we have left. Moreover, because there is no truth outside of myself, there is no other ideal by which to measure these experiences. There is only intensity; some things feel better than others. [35]

Healy vividly describes the loss of a Christian view of life and the consequent difficulty of living without any deeply significant integration point in our contemporary world. He comments:

> With this [the loss of meaning] will come flooding in one or the other—or a cyclic oscillation of the indications of hyperboredom—a deep, mordant indifference or a frenetic search for distraction. . . . [A] vacuum appears at the center of each of us, a shift of perspective so radical that it can hardly fail . . . to produce a bleak, boring sense of nothingness in the wake of this fundamental de-creation. [36]

Healy describes the problem clearly and seems to long for a way to return to a center of some sort. I find few clues about whether or where he finds a center except when he says, "It seems that Man has now to try to grow his roots—such as survive—back into Being, that is, to recover contact with the source of all that he is."[37] However, he makes no attempt to describe this "Being."

I have already quoted Sartre and Nietzsche, the atheistic existentialists who courageously faced the reality of a world emptied of God and recognized that an acute existential awareness of the human predicament may lead to despair or to the search for endless diversions. Other existentialist philosophers who believed in God saw that confronting that boredom might be the road to a deeper and more profound relationship with the creation and the Creator. Better to uncover the mask of diversion and face the emptiness beyond in order to find new meaning. Pascal, Heidegger and Søren Kierkegaard, each in his own way, wrote of the necessity of recognizing the reality of our boredom and seeing the essential nature of reality behind the ordinariness and routine of daily things. The inner emptiness and longing that we all experience from time to time is a sign of something beyond ourselves. In his *Pensées*, Pascal describes the God-shaped vacuum in every person:

> What else does this craving, and this helplessness, proclaim but that there was once in man a true happiness, of which all that now remains is the empty print and trace? This he tries in vain to fill with everything around him, seeking in things that are not there the help he cannot find in those that are, though none can help, since this infinite abyss can be filled only with an infinite and immutable object; in other words, by God himself.[38]

The reality of a personal Being who has created the universe and us for a purpose imbues meaning to every aspect of our busyness. This Christian perspective on life encourages our deep involvement in relationships and our creativity in developing the resources God has given us to enjoy. Every living thing and all art, culture, work and relationships have a deep purpose in reality. As William Shakespeare wrote in the context of the common Christian worldview of his time, most people believed that there was an intrinsic God-given meaning to everything: "tongues in trees, books in the running brooks, / Sermons in stones and good in every thing."[39] This perspective also gives Christians a motive to endure times of tedium and difficulty because they hope in something more beyond this life.

For three hundred years or more, many philosophers and scientists have been urging us to find our own meaning without reference to religion. But in the last twenty years there has been widespread rediscovery and acknowledgment of the importance of religion and spirituality. How we discover "true spirituality" is a huge and vitally important question that is dealt with in many other fine books. I can only encourage my reader to explore the possibility that Christianity might really be true and that it gives a solid foundation and framework for meaning and hope. Although Christianity does not answer all the big questions of life exhaustively, I believe that it answers them in a more satisfactory way than the alternative worldviews or belief systems do. It is the key that unlocks the mystery and makes sense of reality. To believe is not to take a leap in the dark; it is to take a step of faith, based on good reasons. As we have seen, everyone addresses the topic of meaning and purpose from his or her own particular beliefs about reality. No one's position is neutral, and my own foundation and framework have become more obvious, especially in the later chapters of this book.

We have touched on the many different avenues in the search for meaning and hope in recent centuries. Charles Baudelaire, the mid-nineteenth-century French poet, realized that the movement of Romanticism in art and music had failed to lead to a sense of meaning and psychological satisfaction. As a result, the world was boring.[40] So Baudelaire committed himself, in a characteristically intense manner, to the "lust for novelty."[41] In his poem "Le Voyage," he boasts:

> This land wearies us, oh Death, let us sail!
> Even though sky and sea are black as ink
> our hearts you know are filled with light!
> Pour out your poison. . . .
> We want to plunge to the depths of the abyss,
> what matter whether it be Hell or Heaven?—
> to the bottom of the Unknown to find something *new*.

In the next chapter we will explore both the contemporary "lust for novelty" as it is seen in the trivialization of all that is serious, and the relentless and often dangerous search for stimulation and excitement.

11

THE BITTER FRUITS OF BOREDOM
Sexual Addiction, Aggression and Risk Taking

BOREDOM CAN BE A CATALYST THAT SPURS US to activity and interest in new things. For children, learning to tolerate a certain amount of boredom and developing "inner resources" to deal with boredom are part of an important developmental phase. Unfortunately, for most people who encounter boredom, the tendency is to slide into negativity, irritability and self-pity. We live in a time when people do not often complain openly about boredom, yet they are obviously experiencing it as they move restlessly from one form of entertainment to another, searching for new stimulation and for something more than they have already.

The movie *Ghost World* powerfully and disturbingly catches the mood of two teenage girls who have just graduated from high school and are disdainful of following the normal route to college. They drift around in a bleak world of strip malls, thrift stores and 1950s retro diners, cynically and snobbishly observing the people around them, trying to find some entertainment and meaning in the ordinariness of their lives. A restless discontent and boredom pervade their existence, and these are relieved by only the main character's intelligent, black humor.

Experience and intuition are supported by research that has found links between boredom and all sorts of negative states of mind and behavior. We saw earlier that boredom is associated with depression, loneliness, hopelessness, anxiety and hostility. It also has been shown to contribute to pathological gambling, substance abuse and eating disorders.[1] A study of binge eating among college students found that boredom and dissatisfaction with body weight and shape were the most intense feelings just prior to an episode of bingeing.[2] In the field of education there is a correlation between boredom and low grades, poor academic achievement, truancy and early-dropout rates.[3] In the workplace, poor work performance, more frequent accidents and dissatisfaction with the job are associated with boredom.[4] We know that when we are bored, our efficiency and performance are reduced and we are very prone to unhealthy reactions.

We say "the Devil has work for idle hands to do." Kierkegaard asserts "boredom is the root of all evil." "The gods were bored," he continues, "so they created man."[5] Certainly the gods of Greek mythology were often quarreling, and it has been suggested that the Greeks imagined their gods to be like their own leisure class—often bored and "unable to think of any peaceful stimulating activity, [giving] vent to their need for excitement by bickering and quarreling."[6] Eric Hoffer ties boredom to the roots of fanaticism and mass movements:

> There is perhaps no more reliable indicator of a society's ripeness for a mass movement than the prevalence of unrelieved boredom. In almost all the descriptions of the periods preceding the rise of mass movements there is reference to vast ennui; and in their earliest stages mass movements are more likely to find sympathizers and support among the bored than among the exploited and oppressed.[7]

SEDUCED BY SEX

When we are bored, it is easy to give in to more temptation. We find ourselves, for example, like one of my counseling clients, on the slippery slope, the bobsled run, as he called it, of addiction to pornography. His wife was out for the evening, and he stood in the kitchen with money in his pocket, wrestling with the temptation to get in his car and cross the river on the highway, to the part of the city known for its strip clubs. Dennis de Rougemont calls boredom "the hunting reserve of the Demon. Because here *anything* can become tempting, if it is sufficiently intense or exciting, flattering, easy, and a pretext to flee from oneself."[8] In *The Screwtape Letters*, Uncle Screwtape instructs his nephew in the art of seduction:

> My dear Wormwood, . . . In the first place I have always found that the Trough periods of the human undulation provide excellent opportunity for all sensual temptations, particularly those of sex. . . . The attack has a much better chance of success when the man's whole inner world is drab and cold and empty.

He talks about using God-given pleasures to seduce his "patient": "An ever increasing craving for an ever diminishing pleasure is the formula. It is more certain; and it's better *style*. To get the man's soul and give him *nothing* in return—that is what really gladdens Our Father's heart."[9]

A December 8, 1991, *Washington Post* article had the headline "For VA [Virginia] Teens, Emptiness Amid Plenty." As Patricia Spacks remarks, the article reported, " 'Regardless of the money their parents have . . . the clothes, the houses, the cars, the opportunities at school and the proximity to a major city, they say they are bored out of their minds.' [One] high-school senior [said]: 'This is the most boring place I have ever lived.' " The subhead of the article read: "Battling Boredom, Some in the Suburbs Turn to Drinking, Crime."[10]

The Bible's King David was vulnerable to visual enticement and lust when he was alone—and perhaps bored—at a time when normally "kings go off to war" (2 Sam 11:1-2). Away from the excitement of battle, his vulnerability led him into adultery with Bathsheba and, eventually, to having her husband murdered.

We so commonly and so easily turn to sex, food and alcohol—all good gifts of God at the right time and in the right amount—when we are bored and feeling empty. These are rich pleasures given by God but in excess they become like little gods, idols we build our lives around instead of the real thing. Many people turn to food for comfort and stimulation. Cyril Connolly understood this dynamic when he wrote, "Obesity is a mental state, a disease brought on by boredom and disappointment."[11] We know that not all cases of obesity are caused by boredom, but certainly a strong association exists between the two. Boredom is often accompanied by apathy, but it also prompts some people to self-destructive action in an attempt to find some life again, to find some sense of being in control and some relief from discomfort.

Obviously this is a vicious circle for adults and children. A recent report on obesity found that the percentage of children ages six to eleven who are overweight has tripled since the 1960s. One of the reasons is that these children spend many inactive, often half-bored, snack-filled hours in front of the television, where they are exposed to a barrage of fast-food advertising.

"Boredom is a vital problem of the moralist," said philosopher Bertrand Russell, "since at least half the sins of mankind are caused by the fear of it." Rev. Donald McCullough reflects on this "fear" of boredom:

> I'm not sure how we could verify this, but I think he [Bertrand Russell] was accurate. A woman does not wake up in the morning and say, "Oh, it's a perfect day to commit adultery." No, she wakes up to another day where nothing much seems to be happening in her marriage and she finds relief from the wilderness in the oasis of another man's attention; taking one little step after another, she eventually finds herself in a situation she could never before have imagined. Or a man does not set out to be greedy. But to relieve the boredom of business-as-usual at the office, he enters the game, struggles for tangible victories, and before long he is imprisoned in a pattern of grasping for more and more to prove his worth. I imagine boredom was the chief reason the prodigal son left home. Life on the farm has its dreary routines; there are chores to do, day in and day out. And that insufferable brother—boring beyond belief! No wonder he ran off to the far country to squander his substance in riotous living.[12]

PORNOGRAPHY AND BOREDOM

Sex is a wonderful gift that is intended to be expressed and experienced in the context of a lifelong, committed relationship between a man and a woman. Sexual orgasm is one of the most intense pleasures known to human beings. It has the greatest potential of giving us a foretaste of heaven and the greatest potential for leading us toward hell! As is the case with most good things that God has given us to enjoy, we are never satisfied with sexual pleasure and always want more. Most young people begin having sexual relationships in their teen years. Rollo May wrote that "sex has become 'something to do when we can think of nothing to say to each other,' the body is asked to 'compensate for the abdication of the person.' "[13] College students who do not have active sex lives are regarded as strange. Sex is now so casual and ubiquitous that it is no more special than a fast-food pizza. It is accepted as part of the normal social scene along with food, alcohol and drugs. No longer is there the expectation of some level of commitment in the relationship before sexual intercourse. Now the attitude is "What's the big deal about sex? Why not enjoy it with whomever I can and whenever I can?" And most soap operas, teen television shows, magazines, movies and school sex education curricula give the same message. But when sex becomes less mysterious and special, when it is abused and freely available, it has a tendency to become boring.

In every era sex has been used as a "fix" to relieve boredom, to give a sense of taking control and to find release from anxiety, anger and frustration. But because of the technology at hand today, we probably live in the most erotically stimulated culture of all time. We now have the most graphic and extreme forms of pornography available on our computers at the click of a mouse. No longer do you have to risk being seen buying a porn magazine or renting an X-rated video. You can have everything in the privacy of your own room.

The pornography industry is enormous. A few years ago it was estimated that in the United States, 150 hardcore videos were being produced each week. There are twice as many hardcore outlets as there are McDonald's restaurants. There are more than 150,000 porn websites on the Internet, and it is said that the number is growing at a rate of 200 a week. Adult websites are a nearly $1 billion-a-year business with annual growth rates of 20 to 30 percent. In the very near future there will be live strip shows on the Internet with the possibility of sending and receiving stimulating sensations to viewers in their homes. Because of the staggering profitability of pornography, the industry is a major influence on the development of interactive computer, video and DVD technology.[14]

An article in *New York Times* magazine on May 20, 2001, gives a sense of the growth of this industry.

> The $4 billion that Americans spend on video pornography is larger than the annual revenue accrued by either the N.F.L., the N.B.A. or Major League Baseball. But that's literally not the half of it: the porn business is estimated to total between $10 billion and $14 billion annually in the United States, when you toss in the porn networks and pay-per-view movies on cable and satellite, Internet Web sites, in-room hotel movies, phone sex, sex toys and that archaic medium of my own occasionally misspent youth, magazines. . . . People pay more money for pornography in America in a year than they do on movie tickets, more than they do on all the performing arts combined.[15]

Most of this pornography is aimed at men, but there is a growing market for women. The greatest consumers are adolescent boys between the ages of eleven and seventeen. One youth worker told me that when the boys get home from school at 4 p.m., most of them spend two to three hours on the Internet each day, visiting their friends in chat rooms and exploring whatever else they can find. It is frightening to think that this is where most of these boys are being educated about women, sex and "love." And increasingly, young women are watching to find out what men want. Of course, it gives them a very distorted perspective.

THE POISON OF PORNOGRAPHY

Pornography clearly devalues women and makes them merely the objects of sexual pleasure. Most of the images are airbrushed and computer-enhanced, and men who have these images in their minds will find it hard to accept that women, in reality, are not always so "perfect." Many men who have struggled to break free from pornography have told me that they deeply regret having such images in their minds. Ideally sex should be the culmination of intimacy in every other area of life; but in pornography sex is the only thing that matters, and young men may get the idea that this is what love and intimacy are. Pornography also breeds narcissism, a focus on getting what I want rather than in giving to the other person. Love is primarily about giving, lust is about taking. Anna Grear writes:

Pornography is a powerful form of propaganda, promoting sexual worthlessness, sexual trivialization and sexual violence. It takes women, made in the image of God, and distorts their rich personhood into little more than a compilation of sexual parts, to cheapened, panting playthings. Pornography violates. It is a form of violence. It promotes the view that one whole class of persons exists for the use, abuse and entertainment of another. Pornography is a lie.[16]

Why is pornography so much more of a problem for men than for women? It is because of the God-given differences between the sexes and the way in which these good differences have been bent by sin and self-centeredness. Men tend to think about sex a lot more than women do. They are also stimulated by visual images more than women are. It is not wrong to have the God-given enjoyment of the female form, but Jesus clearly taught the difference between looking and lusting. Men also seem to be able to separate sex from relationship more easily. Women usually need time and a loving atmosphere of gentleness and kindness to be able to fully enjoy sex. If they are angry, upset, anxious or afraid, they find it very hard to enjoy physical intimacy beyond holding and cuddling. Men can perform sexually in any mood and without much preparation. Men are more likely to confuse love and lust. Women are more interested in closeness and intimacy, whereas men are more preoccupied with orgasm. In marriage, the greatest fulfillment in sex is often experienced after years of faithfulness in which the spouses have built trust and have grown in their understanding of each other's emotions, thoughts and physical responses.

Women are not immune to the lure of pornography. However, when women become sexually addicted, it is often occurs by feeding fantasies of idealized romantic relationships through magazines and novels. They may use pornography in this context for sexual release. Increasingly I hear of college-age women using pornography to find out how to please a man or to explore lesbian fantasies.

THE POWER, PROGRESSION AND PAIN OF PORNOGRAPHY

The power of pornography lies in its addictive potential. The orgasm, for many people, becomes like a drug "fix." For a few moments it wipes out feelings of pain, anxiety, anger, fear, loneliness and boredom. For those who have learned at an early age to deal with uncomfortable emotional tension by releasing it in an orgasm, pornography will be even more powerfully addictive. Research demonstrates that people who have been abused are more vulnerable to getting hooked. Their sexuality has usually been awakened too early and has been twisted and distorted by abuse.

There is often a progression in the use of pornography. Soft porn images become boring and less stimulating after a while, so increasingly erotic, graphic and often violent images are necessary in order for the viewer to be aroused. An article in *Time* magazine said, "The biggest demand is not for hard-core sex pictures but for 'deviant' material including pedophilia, bondage, sadomasochism and sex acts with various animals."[17]

For the addict there is a progression through magazines, videos, Internet images, phone sex, strip clubs, massage parlors and sex with prostitutes. The tiny seed of the initial choice to open a porn website on the Internet may in a few months or years have developed into a huge tree that is invading every aspect of the person's life. Financial debts may be incurred, marriage problems may escalate, careers may be affected, and divorce and depression may ensue. The pain of pornography is then felt most acutely as self-loathing and shame.

Without any values beyond self-fulfillment and not harming others, many claim that there is nothing wrong with pornography. It does, in fact, harm us and others; and for the Christian, anything that mars the beauty of that for which we were created is harmful. God's commands are for our good and intended for our greatest fulfillment.

For all of us the battle against what Christians call "our sinful nature" is the same. The more we give in to temptation, the more sin will control us. In the early chapters of the Bible we find the story of Cain and Abel. Cain is asked by God to do something, and he wants to do it his way instead of God's way. This is the essence of sin. God says to Cain, "If you do not do what is right, sin is crouching at your door; it desires to have you, but you must master it" (Gen 4:7). Paul picks up this theme in 1 Corinthians, where he talks about the goodness of food and sex. These will give us greatest pleasure if they are enjoyed within the limits of the "Maker's instructions."

In this letter, Paul makes a passionate plea for believers to flee from sexual immorality: "You are not your own; you were bought at a price. Therefore honor God with your body" (1 Cor 6:19-20). We need to hear this message today, in a similarly eroticized culture where desire, pleasure and the search for self-fulfillment are deified. When I walk into the local grocery store and as I stand at the checkout counter, I am faced with magazine covers that urge readers to "Unleash Your Lust" and "Discover His/Her Erogenous Zones," and I remember Paul: "I will not be mastered by anything" (1 Cor 6:12).

I have taken space and time to develop the dangers of pornography because sexual addiction is probably by far the biggest addictive problem in our culture. Alcohol, drugs and gambling all take people down a similar road of self-destruction. All are common escape routes from boredom and difficulty in life.

AGGRESSION AND RISK TAKING

Increased aggression and boredom are certainly linked. The recent spate of shootings in schools in the United States has many causes, but there is a consistent association with alienated young people who have saturated themselves with ideas and images of violence. There has been considerable speculation about the possible influence of the fascinating and very popular movie *The Matrix* on the two young men who, like the characters in the movie, donned black trench coats and gunned down their classmates and teachers at Columbine High School in Littleton, Colorado. Those young adults who struggle with boredom, who harbor feelings of inadequacy and anger, who spend many hours in the world of movies and Internet images, and (in the near future) in highly realistic virtual reality will find it increasingly difficult to separate reality from fantasy. Many teens hang out in the online chat rooms because they openly confess they are bored and that they are looking for some excitement.

The recent murder of two Dartmouth College professors by two teenagers in the normally tranquil state of Vermont has shocked many people. William Anderson, the superintendent of a correctional facility for adolescents in Vermont, said:

I am seeing something in young people coming into jail today I've never seen before. The seventeen-, eighteen-, nineteen-year-old kids I see, they don't care about anything, including themselves. They have absolutely no respect for any kind of authority. They have no direction in their lives whatsoever.[18]

These kids watch a lot of movies and television. Theo Padnos, who teaches literature to incarcerated youth, is deeply committed to this task and is very involved with his students. "They're drawn to the myths built into these violent movies, not just to the violence itself," he says. "These kids half believe that their destination is the same as the screen heroes." In his conversations with them, he hears "the language of apocalypse."

The goal for the bright ones is to truly mesmerize the middle class with violence. They've been transfixed with disaster themselves—in their families, at the movies, in the company of their mentors in crime. They've come to feel that there is nothing out there for them. And so they know exactly the effect they're looking for. They keep up with the news. They read about their deeds in the papers. They've been ignored all their lives, and they're pleased to see that the public is finally giving them some of the attention they're due. . . . The result is just what they'd been hoping for: terrifying, mesmerizing violence, and no context.[19]

In a paper titled "The Intrinsic Appeal of Evil: Sadism, Sensational Thrills and Threatened Egotism," Roy Baumeister and Keith Campbell suggest that for high-sensation-seeking people, the intrinsic appeal of and satisfaction from performing violent acts is the quest for thrilling sensations to escape boredom. The thrill of the illegal activity, rather than any deliberate intention to cause harm, marks this behavior. Baumeister and Campbell quote J. Katz, who found that many shoplifters have little desire for the stolen item. The stories told by these people "focused on what Katz called 'sneaky thrills': the forming of a plan, the concealment of the item, the high suspense of leaving the store with the stolen item, and the euphoric sense of having got away with it."[20]

We have noted the relationship between people who seek high sensation and novelty and a proneness to boredom. Many studies have demonstrated the association between sensation-seeking tendencies and a wide variety of risky behaviors in adolescence, including drug use, reckless driving, delinquency, alcohol consumption, drinking and driving, smoking and risky sex.[21]

A recent study aimed at preventing vehicle crashes at railway crossings found that out of 891 randomly selected residents in Michigan, 10 to 20 percent engaged in extremely dangerous behaviors around rail crossings. Those identified were predominantly males with strong sensation-seeking tendencies: they engaged in new and novel experiences to avoid boredom.[22]

A group of teenagers who have been drinking and using drugs might not intend harm when they cruise the neighborhood, but the situation becomes much more serious when they steal a car and drive recklessly into another car, endangering other people, perhaps badly hurting someone and themselves. A small group of individuals who have a dominant sensation-seeking personality trait and little self control are much more likely to defy the law and seek excitement in drinking, drugs, driving, vandalism, assaulting behavior and other violent crimes.

Baumeister and Campbell describe a horrific incident originally reported by others:

> Two young men, aged 17 and 18, were unable to find anything stimulating to do in the very small town in rural New Jersey where they lived. They walked around, hung out near the bowling alley, and generally felt they had exhausted the meager opportunities to stimulate themselves. They hit on the plan of telephoning pizza places until they found one that would make a late-night delivery to the address they gave, which was an abandoned house in a remote area. When the pizza delivery arrived, the boys shot the drivers to death. They made no effort to rob the pizza employees, and they did not even eat the pizza but simply threw it around.[23]

A final example is the most disturbing. It is the history of the Ku Klux Klan, an organization founded by a small group of six young and intelligent former Confederate soldiers who had no jobs and were very bored. According to a founding member, James Crowe, the Klan's purpose was a social attempt to alleviate their boredom. Their only intention was to "have fun, make mischief, and play pranks on the public."[24] Their costumes were old sheets, raided from the home one of them was house-sitting. Wearing their ghost disguises, they played pranks in the neighborhood. The former slaves became popular targets because they were thought to be largely uneducated, superstitious and gullible. Later, the Klan became notorious for its racial and religious violence: rape, assault, murder and destruction of property. This pattern of gradual degeneration from what, in the beginning, were only "innocent" jokes and pranks for the relief of boredom, into cruelty and evil is not uncommon.

Our exploration of the causes and consequences of boredom has come to an end. In the following final chapters we must find some creative ways to counteract and even cure the universal and common malady of boredom.

12

COUNTERACTING BOREDOM

Six Easy Steps to an Exciting, Never-Bored-Again Life!

SOME TASKS IN LIFE ARE INHERENTLY MONOTONOUS and tedious, and how we approach them is crucial. We can sometimes be like small children who grow easily bored and need help to find things to do. "Boredom Busters for Kids" and The Berenstain Bears with Nothing to Do are just two examples of how to counter childhood doldrums! And for parents facing long summer months ahead, there are the "Best Boredom Busters Under the Sun."[1] My wife was an expert in distracting our children when they became frustrated and bored. As she told our oldest daughter recently, "Parenting small children is basically the art of distraction." Often, when children complain that they are bored, all they want is for a busy parent to stop and sit and talk for a while. They want attention and relationship.

Other times, of course, it is good for children to experience boredom long enough to prompt them to find their own activity and stimulate their creativity. At a two-year-old's birthday party I attended recently, I was struck by the gaudy colors of the many plastic toys covered with knobs to turn, handles to pull and noises to make. These entertained the child for a few moments—the infant equivalent of channel surfing! Simpler, more aesthetically pleasing wooden blocks, an old cardboard box or a pile of stones or leaves in the garden provided more creative challenge and activity and were not abandoned so quickly.

For adults, too, boredom can be a great motivator to action. Patricia Spacks comments that "all 'cultural advance' derives from the need to withstand boredom."[2] She quotes Friedrich Nietzsche, who suggested that men and women of rare sensibility value boredom as an impetus to achievement:

> They do not fear boredom as much as work without pleasure; they actually require a lot of boredom if *their* work is to succeed. For thinkers and all sensitive spirits, boredom is that disagreeable "windless calm" of the soul that precedes a happy voyage and cheerful winds. They have to bear it and must wait for its effect on them. Precisely this is what lesser natures cannot achieve by any means.[3]

For older children this positive aspect of boredom was highlighted in recent article in *Newsweek* by journalist Anna Quindlen, who describes the challenge of long summer vacations:

> How boring it was.
>
> Of course, it was the making of me, as a human being and a writer. Downtime is where we become ourselves, looking into the middle distance, kicking at the curb, lying on the grass or sitting on the stoop and staring at the tedious blue of the summer sky. I don't believe you can write poetry, or compose music, or become an actor without downtime, and plenty of it, a hiatus that passes for boredom but is really the quiet moving of the wheels inside that fuels creativity. And that to me is one of the saddest things about the lives of American children today. Soccer leagues, acting classes, tutors—the calendar of the average middle-class kid is so over the top that soon Palm handhelds will be sold in Toys "R" Us. Our children are as overscheduled as we are, and that is saying something.[4]

Quindlen suggests that it is precisely these times of "doing nothing" when we do our "best thinking, and when creativity comes to call," and that "the overscheduled children of the 21st-century America" are "deprived of the gift of boredom."

Of course, helping children find things to do when they are bored is important. Pets teach us expensive lessons about boredom. A new puppy in our home needed much attention and exercise—or so we learned after he managed to destroy some costly items of clothing and furniture before we were able to find a way to deal with his playful exploratory spirit and boredom. There are often simple, creative and practical solutions to the boredom of young animals or children.

Each day I take this now-adult dog (and he takes me) for a run on the golf course in Forest Park. I get my daily dose of natural beauty as I watch the trees and birds change through the seasons. Sometimes the sunrise over the city is breathtakingly beautiful. I feel much less tired and restless throughout the day, and my dog is far more amenable and relaxed. Those who care for horses know that they need regular exercise to keep them from being unmanageable if they are in a restrictive or boring environment.

I have enjoyed discovering some humorous book titles with quick-fix boredom remedies for adults, such as *The Anti-Boredom Book* and *Dr. Amelia's Boredom Survival Guide: First Aid for Rainy Days, Boring Errands, Waiting Rooms, Whatever!* A travel holiday guide had a feature titled "Cruise Special: The 'I Hate Boredom' Guide—Come Aboard with 30-Plus Instant Vacations. There's Never a Dull Moment." This next one sounds fun: *Ten Sticks of Dynamite: To Blow Up Your Boredom, to Blast Your Mediocrity or Just to Boot You out of Bed.* And if your marriage is dull and needs revitalizing, try this one: "How to Fall in Love (with Him) Again: After Stretches of Boredom, and Even Dislike, You Can Fall in Love All Over Again." And finally, *How to Really Party: The Sure Cure for Boredom* suggests a more dubious solution, one more commonly chosen by college students. These all suggest commonsense ways of dealing with boredom, mostly by recommending things to do. Certainly, as these titles suggest, humor is one way to reduce boredom. However, though you won't find them mentioned in these books, there are some tedious tasks that require us to remember the purpose of seemingly boring activities in the bigger scheme of things.

REMEMBER THE BIG PICTURE

What is the bigger picture that gives meaning and a framework for the smaller, sometimes boring details? When my wife and I wash dishes, vacuum bedrooms or do the laundry, we can get fed up and bored unless we keep in mind the significance of those activities in our marriage and family life.

When I am mowing the lawn for the thirteenth time this year (and mending the mower—again!), I have to remind myself that God created gardens as places of recreation, aesthetic pleasure, social interaction and fruitfulness, and that this is part of my God-given charge to exercise dominion over his world. The attitude with which I wash dishes, do laundry or mow lawns is just as important to God as the attitude with which I go to church or care for my children.

DELIGHT IN THE SIMPLE AND ORDINARY
(OR, STOP AND SMELL THE ROSES)

We need to learn to delight in the simple and ordinary rather than in the extraordinary, dramatic, sensational and exciting. Mary Pipher writes:

> Most real life is rather quiet and routine. Most pleasures are small pleasures—
> a hot shower, a sunset, a bowl of good soup or a good book. Television suggests
> that life is high drama, love and sex. TV families are radically different from
> real families. Things happen much faster to them. On television things that
> are not visually interesting, such as thinking, reading and talking, are ignored.
> Activities such as housework, fund-raising and teaching children to read are
> vastly underreported. Instead of ennobling our ordinary experiences, televi-
> sion suggests that they are not of sufficient interest to document.[5]

In a time when we hear so much about Attention Deficit Disorder, it was intriguing to discover one psychologist writing about Delight Deficiency Disorder! In an article titled "Don't Just Do Something, Sit There," Richard Simon quotes the psychologist Paul Persall, who describes a contemporary syndrome: a cynical set of chronic feelings of anger, irritability, aggression and impatience.

> "A new plague has struck the world." . . . At the root of this plague is the folly
> of worshipping what [Persall] calls "Nowism"—the addiction to technology
> and the instantaneous response, the disconnection from the natural world,
> the final triumph of consumerism and the desperate longing for more and
> more and more. In our headlong rush to keep afloat amid the dizzying pseudo-
> emergencies of our lives . . . we have lost any idea of what it means to live
> wisely.[6]

In his book *Faster: The Acceleration of Just About Everything,* James Gleick writes of our addiction to instant coffee, instant food, instant intimacy, instant sex, instant replay and instant gratification. When McDonald's opened a restaurant in the Piazza di Spagna in Rome in 1986, Carlo Petrini, an Italian journalist, was so enraged that he launched the Slow Food Movement. This movement has now spread to many other countries and aims to resist the homogenization and globalization of food production and consumption, which, they claim, should remain an expression of individual cultures and community life. Another city in Italy, Orvieto, has started *Citta Slow,* or Slow City Movement, to resist the frenetic pace of modern life and to try to keep alive an alternative culture that takes the time to enjoy life's pleasures.

After seeking pleasure in every possible way, the writer of Ecclesiastes concludes that the simple, ordinary, everyday routines of eating, drinking and work—seen in the bigger framework of living in relation to God—bring the deepest enjoyment and satisfaction: "A man can do nothing better than to eat and drink and find satisfaction in his work. This too, I see, is from the hand of God, for without him, who can eat or find enjoyment?" (Eccles 2:24-25; see also 3:12-13).

Meals around family tables, friendships, making music or playing sport together, working at a job—these, all seen in the light of the Creator's bigger purposes, keep us rooted in reality and prevent us from escaping into fantasy. Our little personal stories find their significance and meaning when seen in the context of the Author's story.

CULTIVATING WONDER

The media have so constantly bombarded us with the stimulating and spectacular that our sense of wonder in the life and the world that God has given us has atrophied. It could be argued that even the well-intended National Geographic Society's specials on the wonders of the natural world make my walk in the local park, where I admire the spider's web glistening in the rain or the brilliant fall leaves, a little dull by comparison. The sensationalized nature specials make it harder for my local natural world to live up to the wonders of the Gobi desert or East African game parks. But, of course, these television programs make it possible for the majority of people, who cannot afford to travel, to see these marvelous wonders of the world, and for that I am certainly grateful.

The philosopher René Descartes, writing in 1649, included wonder—meaning intense intellectual interest—as one of the six "passions of the soul." In our own time wonder is replaced on most psychologist's lists of basic emotions by the rather anemic "interest."[7] We jaded adults envy a child's wonder at the caterpillar in the grass, at the fish-eye lens on the world on the tree bud after an ice-storm, at the amazing color and structure in the orchid flower at the botanical garden. Wonder is a capacity we, by effort, must keep alive as a part of the way we are made.

In *The Evidential Power of Beauty* Thomas Dubay says:

> It is troubling that in a universe replete with mind-boggling fascinations masses of people live dull and drab lives. Some are not only apathetic and listless but even insensibly hardened. Biologist Lewis Thomas, who enthusiastically and lucidly shared with the general public his joyous amazement with the living world, was puzzled at the lack of wonder in his scientific colleagues, whose work ought to spark continuing astonishment. "How it happens that today's scientists remain, by and large, such a steady and unruffled lot, writing their cool, meditative papers just as though what they were reporting are the expected, normal, flat facts of the matter, instead of rushing out of their laboratories into the streets shouting their exultation at the queerness of nature, I shall never know."

He also quotes a letter G. K. Chesterton wrote to his future wife: "I do not think there is anyone who takes quite such a fierce pleasure in things being themselves as I do. The startling wetness of water excites and intoxicates me: the fieriness of fire, the steeliness of steel, the unutterable muddiness of mud."[8]

DEVELOPING A PASSION

Psychologists strongly recommend that as an antidote to boredom and aggression, young people develop a particular interest and passion. A passion for art, music, science, sport, horseback riding (something other than videos, television and computers) develops habits of self-discipline and delayed gratification. Often it involves relationships with a teacher, coach or mentor as well as with peers who are also involved in something other than what some psychologists call "second-family values." For many teens the values of their friends and the values portrayed by the media (second-family values) become more important to them than the values of home and parents, "first-family values."[9]

Tibor Scitovsky suggests that teaching peaceful ways to relieve boredom and entertain ourselves is an important part of education.

> A recent survey of U.S. high school teachers showed that they are preoccupied with teaching skills useful for earning income and that they consider leisure skills secondary, with sports the most important of these and the fine arts not even mentioned. Today, teachers seem to consider leisure activities disposable luxuries, not realizing their important function of pacifying and civilizing society.

Later in this article, he continues:

> Moreover, the many hours per day that most teenagers spend in front of a television screen suggest that it displaces not only reading but other leisure activities as well. It does keep boredom at bay during the many hours spent there. But the mental activity of just watching a television screen is so minimal and passive that it is bound not to satisfy the youngsters' need for activity and desire to attract attention and release their energy.[10]

A study of boredom among college students found that the most common way students coped with potentially boring situations was to take a book and read. The students also reported engaging in other activities such as thinking, daydreaming, watching television, being physically active, listening to music and eating.[11]

ACTIVE ENGAGEMENT, NOT JUST PASSIVE EXPECTATION

Finding interest and joy in life involves active engagement with the world. While the passive victim of circumstance will wait in vain, the person who wants to be involved with life knows that it is necessary to move toward someone or something, to *want* to understand and to know. Sloth has been described in theology as a "hatred of all spiritual things that entail effort" and as "faintheartedness in matters of difficulty."[12] Sloth and boredom, as we have seen, often involve a refusal to delight, a loss of wonder and a worship of numbness. Spacks says, "Boredom implies . . . a refusal to pay attention. . . . To focus on any work with intense awareness virtually guarantees finding it interesting—not attractive, necessarily, or admirable, but worthy . . . of the consideration one has given it."[13] Current definitions of *boredom*, such as this one from *The Psychiatric Dictionary*, tend to imply the victim status of the one who is bored: "A feeling of unpleasantness due to a need for more activity, or a lack of meaningful stimuli, or an inability to become stimulated."[14] Some people seem to be better than others at moving into a potentially boring situation, working hard to engage in it and learning something that will help them to find interest in it.

Mihaly Csikszentmihalyi, in "If We Are So Rich, Why Aren't We Happy?" describes the sensation of being fully engaged and engrossed in some activity as the experience of "flow." He says that

> the prerequisite for happiness is the ability to get fully involved in life. . . .
> Our studies suggest that children from the most affluent families find it more
> difficult to be in flow—compared with less well-to-do teenagers, they tend to
> be more bored, less involved, less enthusiastic, less excited.[15]

Perhaps the more affluent teens have not learned the skills or developed the internal resources for dealing with potentially boring situations because they have always had the money for new distracting toys and entertainment.

THE EXPERIENCE OF "FLOW"

In *Flow: The Psychology of Optimal Experience*, Csikszentmihalyi describes how he discovered the principles that can "transform boring and meaningless lives into ones full of enjoyment."[16] He asked people to wear an electronic paging device for a week. The pager sent them a signal eight times a day for a week to remind them to stop and keep a record of what they were thinking and feeling at that time. His research team interviewed thousands of individuals in many cultures around the world, from all walks of life. His earlier studies involved in-depth interviews with a few hundred "experts," surgeons, musicians, chess masters, athletes and artists. From all the material he has gathered over a period of thirty years, he has discovered that there are moments in life that seem to be the exact opposite of boredom. He calls this optimal experience—the experience of flow—an integration and harmony of the body, mind and emotions. My wife and I, in our love for sailing, can identify strongly with one of his examples. "It is what the sailor holding a tight course feels when the wind whips through her hair, when the boat lunges through the waves like a colt—sails, hull, wind, and sea humming a harmony that vibrates in the sailor's veins." My artist daughter identifies with this example: "It is what a painter feels when the colors on the canvas begin to set up a magnetic tension with each other, and a new *thing,* a living form, takes shape in front of the astonished creator."[17]

He found that it is not the things that we usually expect that give the most satisfaction.

> When considering the kind of experience that makes life better, most people first think that happiness consists in experiencing pleasure: good food, good sex, all the comforts that money can buy. We imagine the satisfaction of traveling to exotic places or being surrounded by interesting company and expensive gadgets. If we cannot afford those goals that slick commercials and colorful ads keep reminding us to pursue, then we are happy to settle for a quiet evening in front of the television set with a glass of liquor close by.[18]

These are, of course, enjoyable, but the most rewarding activities are those that are not passive but active, those in which our minds and often our bodies are stretched to their limit "in a voluntary effort to accomplish something difficult and worthwhile."[19]

Optimal experience is described in every culture during a variety of activities, but there are some common ingredients. There is a task or activity (not necessarily physical) for which we have the necessary skills and competence to complete it. If it is too challenging and beyond our abilities, then we feel anxious and threatened. If it is not stretching enough, then we feel bored and restless. When I play tennis with my son-in-law, I feel anxious and incompetent because it is hard to return his powerful shots. He, on the other hand, probably feels bored and unchallenged, although he certainly gets some satisfaction from beating me.

To be highly fulfilling, the task also demands intense concentration, clear goals and immediate feedback. Sailing a fast dinghy in a strong wind is challenging and exhilarating. The immediate goal is to go as fast as one can without capsizing. Downhill skiing is similar in that it requires much concentration and the goal is to negotiate the slope and all its built-in obstacles with as much grace as possible and without falling. Both sports have the added advantage that they usually take place in an environment of great natural beauty.

The task must require intense involvement so that it is impossible to be aware of the normal frustrations and worries of life. When skills and challenges are almost perfectly balanced, one has a feeling of being in control, which is rare in many areas of day-to-day life. Even those who take high risks find their enjoyment not so much in the danger itself but in being able to reduce the risk to levels they can manage.

Often at the time of the task a person is not aware of him- or herself at all, but afterward may have a strong sense of self-confidence and identity. Minutes may seem like hours and hours like a very short time. Csikszentmihalyi gives two more examples:

> A rock climber explains how it feels when he is scaling a mountain: "You are so involved in what you are doing [that] you aren't thinking of yourself as separate from the immediate activity. . . . You don't see yourself as separate from what you are doing."
>
> A mother who enjoys the time spent with her small daughter says: "Her reading is the one thing that she's really into, and we read together. She reads to me, and I read to her, and that's a time when I sort of lose touch with the rest of the world. I'm totally absorbed in what I'm doing."[20]

I can get completely absorbed in my work as a psychotherapist and counselor. I consider it an amazing privilege to be allowed to hear the intimate details of people's life history and inner world. As one of my counseling students said, "I feel as though I am holding this person's heart in my hand." Often it is difficult and painful to hear stories of disappointment, pain and abuse, but it is also wonderful to walk with people, patiently and slowly, as they begin to experience healing. Sometimes I have sat in awe as I have seen the change happening before my eyes.

My brother-in-law is a surgeon, and his experiences of "flow" are very different. The results for him are much more immediate and tangible, and it is hard for him to understand how I could enjoy what I am doing. My brother is a physician and family practitioner, and his experiences are different yet again. Csikszentmihalyi discusses this difference:

> Surgeons who love doing operations claim that they wouldn't switch to internal medicine even if they were paid ten times as much as they are for doing surgery, because an internist never knows exactly how well he is doing. . . . And the surgeon's disdain for psychiatry is even greater than that for internal medicine.[21]

Interestingly people report considerably more experiences of enjoyment at work rather than at leisure, but they also think that there is something wrong with this, that it ought to be the other way around. Surely play should be more pleasurable than work!

> When engaged in leisure activities such as reading, watching TV, having friends over, or going to a restaurant, only 18 percent of the responses ended up in flow. The leisure responses were typically in the range we have come to call *apathy*, characterized by below-average levels of both challenges and skills. In this condition, people tend to say that they feel passive, weak, dull, and dissatisfied.[22]

The key is being actively involved and using highly developed abilities. "The flow experience that results from the use of skills leads to growth," says Csikszentmihalyi. "Passive entertainment leads nowhere."

> Unless a person takes charge of them, both work and free time are likely to be disappointing. Most jobs and many leisure activities—especially those involving the passive consumption of mass media—are not designed to make us happy and strong. Their purpose is to make money for someone else. If we allow them to, they can suck out the marrow of our lives, leaving only feeble husks.[23]

I am very grateful to a friend who took me bird watching on the coast of Norfolk after my medical school final exams. We lay on cold, damp dikes at five in the morning to watch the waders on the shore. I was bitten by an enthusiasm for the beauty of birds and began to listen in a new way. Now when I walk I hear the individual bird songs and am eager to identify the source of the sound. But it has taken years of learning and practice to get to a point where the times of boredom and frustration are much less frequent than they were. Gardening is the same for me. In my youth, I used to despise gardening. *How boring,* I thought. Now my wife and I love creating a place of beauty in our garden, but we are still learning what grows where and when.

Cooking is a necessary part of life, but many find it very boring and easily opt for prepared or frozen foods. It takes time and effort to study cookbooks, to learn how to prepare different vegetables or meats in the best way. But there is such satisfaction in working with an amazing variety of colors, textures and smells to produce a meal that gives pleasure to others. Meals should be more than filling our stomachs with food. They are opportunities to spend time with other people, to have conversations about the day's events and challenges, to share our stories, tears and laughter.

For those of the current generation the normal reflex when bored is to watch a video or surf the Web. What can we do to help our young people accept the short-term pain of learning creative life skills in order to avoid the long-term pain of chronic subconscious boredom and addiction to electronic entertainment that will shrivel their souls? Many of the short-term solutions to boredom, such as television or drugs, undoubtedly give pleasure. But these are unsustainable and provide only a counterfeit of life and ultimately lead to spiritual emptiness.

In God's creation we can find so much to take an interest in, but it takes effort and self-discipline for us to stop long enough to look and marvel at the structure of a flower or a leaf, to wonder how long it took a mountain to form, to see reflections in the smallest puddle, to watch the wind blowing seeds from a flower, to want to know what each snowflake looks like, to marvel that our nails and hair and skin are constantly growing, to learn the names of birds and trees or to learn to listen to bird songs. Elizabeth Barrett Browning's poem "Aurora Leigh, Seventh Book" expresses something of this:

> Earth's crammed with heaven,
> And every common bush afire with God;
> But only he who sees, takes off his shoes—
> The rest sit round it and pluck blackberries.

Sloth is a "refusal to be moved, and to be moved especially to any real endeavor, by contemplation of the good and the beautiful."[24] Pipher says that students who are raised on television "can identify twenty kinds of cold cereal but not the trees and birds in their neighborhoods."[25]

One crosscultural study of boredom proneness and time structure found that American students were characterized by significantly greater boredom than Irish students because of their inability to keep themselves interested and entertained.[26] Here again is suggestive empirical evidence of the "shriveling of inner resources" in a generation dominated by materialism, television and Hollywood. It is probably merely a matter of time before the Irish students have the same problem.

We are called to celebrate and protect the good and beautiful. The wise words of Dubay are a fitting end to this chapter:

> If healthy infants begin life with an inquisitive interest in their surroundings and then grow to delight in attractive sights and sounds and experiences, how does existential boredom come about? Causal explanations are probably complex in most cases: an unhappy home life, little real love, few experiences of nature and art, a poor education, devoid of fostering a sense of wonder. Parents who are innerly empty, and themselves poverty stricken when it comes to a sense for radiant loveliness, cannot give what they themselves lack. Teachers content with communicating mere facts, and who themselves never thrill at what they teach (even mathematics can be exciting!), are hardly going to stimulate their students. Dullness begets dullness.
>
> But probably the chief cause of jadedness is a satiation, a surfeit born of a hedonistic immersion in sensual gratification, together with avarice and pride. A lifestyle of selfish egoism and continuing dissipation progressively deadens an excitement with reality born of innocence and solid virtue, self-denial, and genuine love.[27]

13

NOT SO EASY, NOT SO FAST

Some Foundational Themes of Life

THOUGH WE ARE TEMPTED by the ever-present, seductive quick fix, most of us have discovered that lasting solutions to the serious problems of life usually take patience and require evaluation of some foundational principles and themes. In dealing with boredom we need to consider the importance of leisure, the pursuit of happiness and the problem of knowing what is good and beautiful in a world dominated by relativism.

CULTIVATING TRUE LEISURE

There is a time to be lazy, a time to slow down, a time to play, a time to reflect on the world around us and the world inside us. Often we are afraid to "be still" because the endless distractions of busyness and entertainment keep us from having to face fundamental questions about our existence and about our deeper anxieties, insecurities and fears. We are literally running from ourselves. Josef Pieper wrote a book some years ago called *Leisure: The Basis of Culture*. The jacket of the current edition carries this affirmation: "This book issues a startling warning: Unless we regain the art of silence and insight, the ability for nonactivity, unless we substitute true leisure for our hectic amusements, we will destroy our culture—and ourselves."[1] Pieper argues that leisure is not just distraction and entertainment but a time of withdrawal from the ordinary routines to renew our priorities and our perspective on life. Without it we will not see reality truly. Similarly, writer and lecturer Os Guinness distinguishes sloth

> from idling, a state of carefree lingering that can be admirable, as in friends lingering over a meal or lovers whiling away hours in delighted enjoyment. In W. H. Davies's lines, "What is this life, if full of care, / We have no time to stand and stare?" Or as George MacDonald argued, "Work is not always required of a man. There is such a thing as sacred idleness, the cultivation of which is now fearfully neglected."[2]

In this fast-paced culture we find it hard to slow down and be still. Even our leisure times often get packed with endless activities. "Perhaps you can judge the inner health of a land by the capacity of its people to do nothing," wrote Sebastian de Grazia in 1962, "to lie abed musing, to amble about aimlessly, to sit having a coffee—because whoever can do nothing, letting his thoughts go where they may, must be at peace with himself."[3] The biblical command to rest for one day of the week is an important God-given principle for our health and sanity. We neglect it at our peril. Some people feel very guilty if they are not doing something "worthwhile" with their time. They cannot rest with a clear conscience. The Christian understanding of the sabbath is that it is given by God as a symbol of our being able to rest in his presence with easy consciences. Knowing that we are forgiven and accepted by him, we do not have to work to earn our salvation because Christ has done all that was necessary for us to have a relationship with him. We can, as the Bible says, "enter God's rest" (Heb 4:1-11). We need to take time for our minds and bodies to re-create and recover from being driven so hard. This also allows time for a renewal of perspective.

Leisure time is often when we rest and relax, but it is also good for us to know how to play well. We live in a time when entertainment comes to us while we watch, and though that is not all bad, it is important for us to engage in active as well as passive play. We listen to music, we watch sports on television, we go to movies—but how often do we make music? How often do we get out and play a sport ourselves or go hiking, climbing, biking or sailing?

Some people think of Christians as being joyless and sober, suspicious of any earthly pleasures and preoccupied with spiritual things, of being too heavenly minded to be any earthly good. On the contrary, when truly understood, Christianity sets us free to enjoy leisure and pleasure in the way God originally intended. It affirms the goodness of the creation, of food, of drink, of beauty. But it does restrain us when we tend to go to excess and make gods out of these pleasures.

IS THE PURSUIT OF HAPPINESS THE ANTIDOTE TO BOREDOM?

For many people the main question in life is, What will make me happy? The implication behind this question is that if we can discover the secret to happiness then we will not be miserable or bored. In a survey at the University of Michigan, people were asked what would improve the quality of their lives. One answer stood out above the others: more money. In poor countries, having money to meet basic needs for food, shelter and social contact does make people happier. But beyond that, in countries where most people can afford basic necessities of life, there is a very weak correlation between income and happiness.[4] The more people have, the more they want. Most of us evaluate our possessions and lifestyles by comparing ourselves with those who have more than us. We cannot deny that money does bring some happiness and is very convenient and helpful, but it too easily dominates our lives. Mihaly Csikszentmihalyi writes, "As is true of addiction in general, material rewards at first enrich the quality of life. Because of this, we tend to conclude that more must be better. But life is rarely linear; in most cases, what is good in small quantities becomes commonplace and then harmful in larger doses." There are hidden costs that do not become apparent immediately. Csikszentmihalyi comments that as people become increasingly materialistic, their "sensitivity to other reward" begins to "atrophy."[5] They become bored with things that are not immediately connected to making or spending money.

Friendship, art, literature, natural beauty, religion and philosophy become less and less interesting. The Swedish economist Stephen Linder was the first to point out that as income and, therefore, the value of one's time increases, it becomes less and less "rational" to spend it on anything besides making money—or on spending it conspicuously.[6] The economic cost of playing with one's child, reading poetry or attending a family reunion become too high, and so one stops doing such irrational things. Eventually a person who only responds to material rewards becomes blind to any other kind and loses the ability to derive happiness from other sources.[7]

Happiness, we discover, is usually a byproduct of other things. When pursued directly it often proves elusive. But it can be found when we pursue goodness and beauty.

KNOWING "THE GOOD AND THE BEAUTIFUL"

The problem now becomes, how do we know what is truly good and beautiful, in order to pursue it? Let me take you on a slightly complicated diversion with this important philosophical question, because it has enormous practical implications. To many people a sense of what is good and bad is self-evident. Allowing for an enormous diversity of taste, there are some things at the core of our day-to-day experience that are self-evidently, pragmatically and aesthetically good and beautiful. Throughout the world, with some cultural variations, there is a commonly agreed on recognition of beauty in the face of a woman. So too most cultures agree that murdering someone is wrong. But increasingly, people who have been influenced by the relativism of contemporary philosophers are discarding any externally imposed or externally given standard of aesthetics or morals and are instead turning to a subjective standard. Philosopher Jerome Neu sees a direct connection between this phenomenon and boredom as he points out the historical shift from an objective definition of *good* to a subjective and emotional one. The latter may be stated simply: If something makes me happy or if I like it, I call it good—I define what is good.[8]

Neu himself seems to favor Aristotle's pragmatic idea that something is good if it fulfills its intended function well. He uses the example of a clock keeping time and thus being a good clock. This standard may be fine for clocks because we know what they were intended to do, but the history of psychology and sociology is evidence that we are not so sure what we human beings are designed to be and do. Neu, in reflecting on the standards of goodness and beauty, asks:

To be objective, must they be universal? Are some things objectively good, objectively desirable in a way that makes life (interestingly, joyfully, or merely dutifully) worth living? And again, are some things objectively bad in a way that makes them intolerably boring, killing any interest in them if not in life?[9]

Neu acknowledges that this question takes us to the heart of the matter: "So, once again the quest for an understanding of boredom makes one feel the need for a larger theory of human nature, an understanding of the cycles of desire and fulfillment, of pleasure and attention."[10]

Do our desires and longings reflect an underlying pattern and design of what we are made for, or are they infinitely malleable and changeable according to the culture and the time in history? The question as Neu puts it succinctly is: "What should they (we) want?"[11]

If there is a Creator who has designed us to live in a particular way in order to be the most fulfilled, then the "should" is very relevant. The "should" helps direct our longings and desires toward God and what he values. He builds into our hearts an aesthetic and moral compass that guides us to what is good and beautiful and that helps us discern what is bad and ugly. Fulfillment will come as we live the way our Creator intended us to live.

If, however, we are here as products of millions of years of chance and evolution, then there is no "should" or "ought," there is only what "is." We are left with nothing more than the subjective and pragmatic. The Christian perspective on life gives a framework of meaning that helps us to see value and purpose in the big and the small things of life. It enables us to make the distinctions we have been struggling toward: distinctions between dignity and depravity, beauty and brokenness, grief and glory. If it is in the end the framework of meaning that deeply affects whether events appear interesting or boring, then a renewal of one's perspective, by any means possible, is crucial.

Someone who has a hard time making such distinctions and who is bored with life is likely to be unmoved by the suffering and ugliness that is all around us. We are creatures of great dignity but also terrible depravity. We have amazing glory but also experience great grief. There is so much beauty but also heart-wrenching brokenness. How can someone remain unmoved by this? William May writes about the medieval sin of sloth:

Perhaps boredom is the best modern term to characterize this deadness of the soul. . . . Although the modern sophisticate feels no need to apologize for being bored—his attitude, after all, merely reflects the poverty of his object—the man of faith must confess his boredom as his sin because his attitude reflects the poverty of his own soul. To be unmoved and untouched in the presence of God [and I would add, his creation] exposes an interior inadequacy.[12]

The extraordinary beauty of so much of the universe—its simplicity, harmony and, at the same time, amazing complexity—points to the reality of the existence of a Creator. John Calvin wrote of the "wisdom of God" who designated "this magnificent theater of heaven and earth crammed with innumerable miracles" for us to contemplate and thus to know the Creator.[13] King David speaks of this in Psalm 19:1-2:

The heavens declare the glory of God;
    the skies proclaim the work of his hands.
Day after day they pour forth speech;
    night after night they display knowledge.

The apostle Paul writes, "For since the creation of the world God's invisible qualities—his eternal power and divine nature—have been clearly seen, being understood from what has been made, so that men are without excuse" (Rom 1:20).

REFLECT ON AND REFLECT THE CHARACTER OF GOD

Is God sitting back, feeling bored with his creation? From all that we read in the Scriptures, it seems that he feels very deeply about all that he has made—it is good. Every day he is delighted and excited to make the sun rise and the moon set and to sustain all life. In the biblical story of Job, God challenges Job to trust him even when in great grief and pain, he asks Job questions to contrast the greatness of the Creator and his delight in what he has made to Job's smallness and finiteness:

Do you know when the mountain goats give birth?
    Do you watch when the doe bears her fawn?
Do you count the months till they bear?
    Do you know the time they give birth? . . .

Look at the behemoth [a large animal, possibly a hippopotamus],
    which I made along with you
    and which feeds on grass like an ox.
What strength he has in his loins,
    what power in the muscles of his belly! . . .
He ranks first among the works of God. (Job 39:1-2; 40:15-16, 19)

There is a rhythm and order to the creation—a repetition of grand themes in the cycles of nature, in the patterns in the trees and flowers and in the migratory habits of the salmon and the arctic tern. G. K. Chesterton reflected on the possible monotony of God's daily round and task:

> [Children] always say, "Do it again"; and the grown-up person does it again until he is nearly dead. For grown-up people are not strong enough to exult in monotony. But perhaps God is strong enough to exult in monotony. It is possible that God says every morning, "Do it again" to the sun; and every evening, "Do it again!" to the moon. It may not be automatic necessity that makes all daisies alike; it may be that God makes every daisy separately, but has never got tired of making them. It may be that He has the eternal appetite of infancy; for we have sinned and grown old, and our Father is younger than we.
>
> There is a wondrous diversity in the creation, and as we explore the world of plants, trees, birds, butterflies . . . we cannot help but be awed by the magnificence of it all. But it is hard to avoid the ugliness and evil.[14]

Recently I went with my (adult) daughter to see *The Thin Red Line,* a harrowing two-and-a-half-hour film about an episode in the Second World War in the Pacific. As we (the viewers) are in the tall grass with the small group of men who are waiting for the signal to attack a heavily fortified Japanese bunker on the hill above, with only a small chance of coming out alive, the camera moves from the sweating, terrified face of a young soldier to the blade of grass right in front of him, on which is perched a most beautiful butterfly. In the background are the audible thoughts of one of the soldiers; he asks how—in the presence of such glory as the loyalty, love and heroism of human beings and the stunning beauty of butterflies, birds and flowers—human beings could also be so ugly and barbarous to each other. He sees a "war at the heart of nature." He asks, "The great evil, where did it come from? How did it steal into the world? What root did it grow from?" Later he says, "One man looks at a dying bird [and] . . . sees death is going to have the final word, laughing at him. Another man looks at that same bird and sees the glory—something shining through."[15]

This raises one of the hardest questions we all face. If there is a God, we are tempted to think that he must be a cosmic sadist to allow such terrible ugliness and evil. But the Bible tells us of a God who enjoys the beauty and glory of what he has made; yet, every day he also grieves over the sinfulness, ugliness and brokenness that has come into the world. The Bible tells us that his heart was full of pain as he saw the rapid and terrible spread of evil over the face of the earth (Gen 6:6).

The Creator is a God of passion, with a full range of pure emotions. He is also a God of compassion, suffering for people and with them. We have seen how King David expresses a wide range of feelings in the psalms. At times David is full of worship, joy and thankfulness, while at other times he is in the depths of despair or grief. Perhaps our worship would reflect more of the heart of God if we used the laments as well as the "happy" psalms. If we are to reflect his character we cannot remain unmoved, untouched and bored with him or his creation. Often we have a very underdeveloped sense of his glory and our sinfulness. We are to be people of deep feeling and passion, aware that our feelings need to be redeemed from their distortion and deadness and given full rein in the service of their Maker.

Some have grown bored after experiencing dry, legalistic churches where there is orthodox teaching but little life, love or laughter. At the other end of the spectrum, others have found churches with plenty of excitement, entertainment and emotion where there is little good teaching but everyone has a great time. I recently noticed one church called Exciting First Baptist.

Of course our emotions should be involved in worship, but too often we want peace and happiness like an emotional fix. We want instant pain relief and entertainment. When God does not come through like that, we manufacture techniques and teaching to give us the excitement and experience we crave. Worship has to be ever more entertaining and thrilling.

At first everything is wonderful, but after a time there is an ever-increasing desire for something more—another gift of the Spirit, another healing miracle, more dramatic experiences in worship.

But the Bible does not promise complete happiness, health, wealth or dramatic experiences of God's presence until we are in glory (i.e., heaven). Christian maturity involves learning to delay gratification, to groan, to rejoice in hope and to wait eagerly and patiently for the complete fulfillment of God's many promises of restoration and renewal (Rom 8:22-27). God does indeed offer something deeper and more fulfilling now and in the future, but these are not often associated with the instant thrills and excitement promised by the culture of advertising and entertainment. Sensation seekers and the instant-fix generation often have a hard time with that, and they may end up disappointed and bored with God.

GLORY RESTORED

The Westminster Confession says that the purpose of life is to "love God and enjoy him for ever." Glorifying God means loving him. It also means that we love what he has made and seek to serve him by using the gifts he has given us. He wants us to love the ordinary as well as the extraordinary. Remember the wonderful line in the movie *Chariots of Fire* when Eric Liddel says, "When I run, I feel God's pleasure."[16] He was so caught up with developing a skill that God had given him that he had little time to feel bored. He saw every aspect of his life as spiritual and knew it was meant to be enjoyed before the face of the Creator. We are creatures who, because we are made in the image of God, have a glory of our own. God wants us to be as fully human as we can be, to live out our glory. He wants us to develop our gifts and capacities and use them to the full. I see the "glory" of my black retriever as he streaks across the field yet again in pursuit of a ball, returning with it, his pleading eyes asking me to throw it once more. I see the glory of the eagle in flight, and I see the glory of my friend who is a percussionist for the symphony as he moves easily around the stage among the rest of the orchestra, playing more than thirty instruments in a stunning percussion concerto. I see the glory in my artist daughter as she works on a canvas. I see the glory in my wife as she uses the flowers of God's creation to decorate for parties and weddings and bring joy to special moments of celebration. I think of the glory of highly intelligent doctors and scientists, such as Louis Pasteur, who saved millions of lives with his discovery of penicillin.

Samuel Johnson, writing in the eighteenth century, did not believe that boredom (he did not use that word) was even possible for

curious creatures such as ourselves. "To be born in ignorance with a capacity for knowledge," he wrote, "and to be placed in the midst of a world filled with variety, perpetually pressing upon our senses and irritating curiosity, is surely sufficient security against"—and here no simple word came to his mind— "the languishment of inattention."[17]

God not only wants me to fully use whatever musical, artistic, intellectual, athletic and creative gifts I have, but he also wants to transform my character and make me more like him. My glory is marred and distorted by sin, and throughout my life he is in the process of changing me, using all sorts of circumstances. The apostle Paul says, "We, who . . . all reflect the Lord's glory, are being transformed into his likeness with ever-increasing glory" (2 Cor 3:18).

Not only are we to reflect and enhance the glory of being made in God's image, but we are called to a redemptive task. We are to work against sin in every area of our life. In any part of life where the destructive power of sin has taken hold, it will take effort and prayer to reverse the trend. As Edmund Burke said many years ago "The only thing necessary for the triumph of evil is for good men to do nothing." Resignation, apathy and boredom invade when we feel hopeless and helpless (and often hostile). With such an attitude we have no desire to create a place of beauty out of ugliness, a place of order out of chaos. When we catch a glimpse of the big picture, where our story fits with God's, we are motivated to action.

Engagement with life is not a comfortable path, but neither is it a boring interstate that bypasses life. The test of our spirituality is neither in our best clothes nor in our religious settings but in our response to the everyday and the unavoidable. The test is in our ability to bring good out of hardship and joy out of the mundane. As we shall see in the final chapter, when we begin to grasp the real nature of the struggle of this life, the drama sharpens and the details take on extraordinary significance.

14

WHY GET UP IN THE MORNING?

Boredom and the Battle

BILBO BAGGINS, J. R. R. TOLKIEN'S FAMOUS HOBBIT, could have stayed at home in his comfortable little house and his garden. The Bagginses were, after all, "very respectable. . . . They never had any adventures or did anything unexpected."[1] But when Gandalf the wizard came to call one memorable day, Bilbo sensed that something big was at stake. He was needed in the great (and as yet almost invisible) battle between good and evil. On the ensuing journey he faced many dangers and challenges, but his life was certainly never so boring as it might have been had he stayed home!

Like Bilbo, we are called to an adventure—to a battle with evil for truth, love and life, and to deep, often complicated but wonderful relationships with God and with the men, women and children in our lives. Author John Eldredge sees most men in the church as having been conditioned to be kind and really nice—gentle and kind but bored and boring. They have lost a sense of adventure, and they have little awareness of the battles to be fought. He points to many passages in the Bible that portray God as a warrior going into battle.[2] In the footsteps of Jesus, who was far from being just "gentle, meek and mild," we are not to be people who just pursue our own fulfillment and pleasure but—in the words of the prophet Isaiah that Jesus applied to himself—we are to be people who "preach the good news to the

poor," "bind up the brokenhearted," "proclaim freedom for the captives,"
"comfort all who mourn," "provide for those who grieve," and

> bestow on them a crown of beauty
> instead of ashes,
> the oil of gladness
> instead of mourning,
> and a garment of praise
> instead of a spirit of despair. (Is 61:1-3)

Both men and women are called to fight in the battle against "the world,
the flesh and the devil," resisting evil and sin whether we find it in our own
hearts or in the world around us.

My thesis in these final chapters is that to some degree we all have lost
sight of what we are made for and have been seduced and brainwashed by
the culture and often, sadly, by the church too. We can no longer see the
drama of the bigger picture of life, where so much is at stake. We are called
to an adventure of life with the true and knowable God that may have its
profoundly frustrating and boring moments but that gives meaning to a life
in which every situation has significance.

Dennis de Rougemont writes, "When I hear someone saying, with a
yawn, 'What am I to do—I'm no longer interested in anything?' " he is reminded of Kierkegaard's response to a similar question in which he told the
person to take any Christian commandment and try to practice it in his life.

> For it is clear that this effort, if it be sincere, will reintroduce you into reality,
> where the true conflicts manifest themselves, where the lines of force of the
> spiritual or moral life appear, where the drama of a calling instantly sharpens:
> not even a second of boredom becomes possible any longer. And your com-
> plaint will be that you have only one life to lead.[3]

We are called not only to enjoy the world of God's creation but also to
love our neighbors as we love ourselves. Throughout the Bible we find a
strong emphasis on serving others. One of the reasons why boredom has become so much more common is because we have become too preoccupied
with looking after ourselves, making sure our needs are met, and to put it
bluntly, we have become too selfish. John Ortberg says:

Ironically, often the thing that keeps me from experiencing joy is my preoccupation with *self*. The very selfishness that keeps me from pouring myself out for the joy of others also keeps me from noticing and delighting in the myriad of small gifts God offers each day. This is why Walker Percy describes boredom as the "self *stuffed with the self*."[4]

MADE FOR MORE: THE FRUSTRATIONS OF FALLENNESS

We will always be frustrated and irritated with this imperfect world. While we are made with deep longings for meaning and fulfillment, those longings cannot be satisfied completely on this side of heaven. We face monotony, drabness, waiting in long lines, twelve-hour car journeys and long illnesses. Some have to endure extremes of sensory deprivation in a hospital bed, lying for hours in one position, perhaps staring at the ceiling. Others have been locked in tiny prison cells, cut off from nature and most human contact for years on end.

We live in the shadow of the Fall, with the results of sin. Part of the judgment for Adam and Eve's sin was that they would have to fight against thorns and thistles, which would frustrate their gardening and farming activity. Weeding a large vegetable patch can be a tiring, frustrating and boring business. You have to do it again and again. We confront frustration and tedium as we push back the effects of sin in any area of life. It often feels as if the weeds, the rust, the moths, the dust, the bacteria, the mold and the cancer are winning despite our using every means at our disposal to push back their encroachment yet again. We have a built-in, God-given longing to be free from the Sisyphean tasks of life. We groan, Paul says, with the whole of creation, like a mother in childbirth, longing to be free from the pain of labor, eagerly and patiently awaiting the day when it will be all over and we will be set free (Rom 8:22-25). We are constantly restless, desiring something we do not yet have.

LONGING FOR "THE DAY"

When we looked at the different types of boredom earlier, we noted that part of the experience is "the nagging desire for *something*, the nature of which is forever hidden."[5] It is not just the lack of something we want to do but a dissatisfaction that points beyond itself to something we cannot even describe. Philosopher Arthur Schopenhauer wrote of a "fearful ennui that paralyses life, vain yearning without a definite object."[6] Perhaps his yearning reflected the reality of something beyond this life he did not believe in but for which he was made by his Creator.

There is so much that is good in our world, but it is not enough to fully satisfy us. We were made for more. C. S. Lewis puts it well:

> These things—the beauty, the memory of our own past—are good images of what we really desire, but if they are mistaken for the thing itself, they turn into dumb idols, breaking the hearts of their worshippers. For they are not the thing itself; they are only the scent of a flower we have not found, the echo of a tune we have not heard, news from a country we have never yet visited.[7]

The prophet Malachi looks forward to the day of Christ's return and imagines it as a day of fulfillment and of great freedom from restraint. The picture he uses was made vivid for me during one winter as I walked through the Swiss mountain villages where the village farmers live in beautiful old chalets built into the sides of steep mountains. The basements of most of these chalets are often used as stables for the farmer's cattle, and here the animals are kept during the long winter months. In the spring there comes a day when the snows of winter have begun to melt on the high pastures and the cows are released from their captivity; they go running and bucking through the narrow streets, with bells jangling around their necks, to roam the mountainsides in the warm sunlight. The prophet Malachi writes of "the day of the Lord" when the terrible judgment of God on evil and arrogance will come. He contrasts that judgment day with another day, when "for you who revere [the Lord's] name, the sun of righteousness will rise with healing in its wings. And you will go out and leap like calves released from the stall" (Mal 4:2). Imagine the tedium, weariness and ennui of being shut up in a little stable all winter. And then imagine the joy, the exhilaration of being set free!

You have, no doubt, seen the great lions and tigers in the zoo pacing their cages for hours on end. Watching them for any length of time, we realize that they were made for more. While zoos are fun, they often disturb my children and me; we have a deep sense that something is wrong with keeping the animals from their natural habitat and freedom. We want to set them free and would prefer to see them living the way they were intended to live. The human situation is similar. Until the day comes when we are set free from the restrictions and bondage of a fallen world, we are called to be faithful in every small task that the Lord gives us. You are called to "love the Lord your God with all your heart and with all your soul and with all your mind, . . . [and] love your neighbor as yourself" (Mt 22:37-39). If we could catch the full implications of this, we would find no time to be bored. Remember the John Berryman poem that begins

> Life, friends, is boring. We must not say so.
> After all, the sky flashes, the great sea yearns,
> we ourselves flash and yearn. . . .

We might say that God flashes in glory, love and anger and yearns for the redemption of all creation. We are to be like him!

NO YAWNING

Gerard Manley Hopkins's poem "God's Grandeur" expresses very clearly and beautifully the two sides of the world in which we live: the "grandeur" and the grind.

> The world is charged with the grandeur of God.
> It will flame out, like shining from shook foil;
> It gathers to a greatness, like the ooze of oil
> Crushed. Why do men then now not reck his rod?
> Generations have trod, have trod, have trod;
> And all is seared with trade; bleared, smeared with toil;
> And wears man's smudge and shared man's smell: the soil
> Is bare now, nor can foot feel, being shod.
> And for all this, nature is never spent;
> There lives the dearest freshness deep down things;
>
> And though the last lights off the black West went
> Oh, morning, at the brown brink eastward, springs—

Because the Holy Ghost over the bent
World broods with warm breast and ah! bright wings.

We see the "grandeur" and glory of God's creation, and yet we are also deeply aware of the weariness of the daily grind in a world that is "bleared, smeared with toil." Here we choose to keep treading, generation after generation, in the footsteps of our ancestors, sustained by the hope and belief that there is more in the "deep down things," and in the brooding presence of the Spirit of God, that will one day give new life to the world and banish the boring moments forever.

Lest I weary you with a never-ending and boring book, I must draw the threads of these last few points together. We are called, first, to contemplate the character of God and his creation; second, to confess getting our priorities wrong and pursuing of false gods; third, to creatively counteract some of the tedious and boring tasks of life; and finally—and this is a topic we have only touched on in earlier chapters—to find the help and companionship we need from those in our community. We cannot fight this battle alone. We need fellow travelers to walk with us.

Os Guinness writes well of the call of God:

> Personally summoned by the Creator of the universe, we are given a meaning in what we do that flames over every second and inch of our lives. Challenged, inspired, rebuked, and encouraged by God's call, we cannot for a moment settle down to the comfortable, the mediocre, the banal, and the boring. The call is always to the higher, the deeper, and the farther. . . . In short, every time the marsh gas of sloth rises from the swamps of modern life and threatens to overcome us, the call of God jerks us wide awake. Against the most sluggish temptation to feel "Who cares?" calling is the supreme motivation, the ultimate "why." God has called us, and we are never more ourselves than when we are fully stretched in answering. There is no yawning in response to this call.[8]

TO SURF OR TO SERVE?

Ultimately we are faced with a choice. We can choose to surf the channels, the Web or the waves in order to try to satisfy our desire for "something more," our craving for the next exciting fix to make us feel alive and to relieve our boredom. Or we can choose to respond to the call to love and serve the true and living God who promises to satisfy our pangs of hunger and to quench our deepest thirst for meaning and significance. He is the one who gives us a reason to delight in his world and a passion for living. He is the one who helps us patiently endure the inevitable moments of frustration and boredom. As we live in a relationship with him and in the light of what he has told us about the world and what we are to desire, our perspective on the often difficult and boring is, day by day, little by little, transformed. As we see things more and more from God's point of view, we find there is rarely time to be bored!

NOTES

Introduction

[1]Darren Star, "Post 9/11: The Series. An Interview with Lynn Hirschberg," *New York Times Magazine*, November 11, 2001, pp. 118-19.

[2]Patricia Meyer Spacks, *Boredom: The Literary History of a State of Mind* (Chicago: University of Chicago Press, 1995), p. 272.

Chapter 1: Three Yawns for Boredom!

[1]Yankelovich Partners market research study of consumer attitudes (2000), quoted in Tom Kuntz, "Yawn: These Are Such Exciting Times," *New York Times*, February 20, 2000, p. WK 7.

[2]Judson Gooding, "How to Cope with Boredom," *Reader's Digest*, February 1976, p. 51.

[3]Rowan Williams, "You're Bored, Damned Bored," *The Sunday Times* (London), March 31, 2002, p. 3.

[4]Reinhard Kuhn, *The Demon of Noontide: Ennui in Western Literature* (Princeton, N.J.: Princeton University Press, 1976), p. 7.

[5]Bernice Kanner, "Hungry or Just Bored," *American Demographics* 28, no. 1 (1999): 15. (Data based on 315 responses to a poll conducted in August 1998 by Cyber Dialogue, a New York-based online research firm.)

[6]The "apathetic" and "interesting" lists come from *Roget's 21st Century Thesaurus in Dictionary Form*, ed. Barbara Ann Kipfer (New York: Dell, 1992).

[7]*Webster's New World Dictionary College Dictionary*, 4th ed. (New York: Macmillan, 1999), p. 169.

[8]Ambrose Bierce, *The Devil's Dictionary* (1906; reprint, New York: Oxford University Press, 1999), p. 19.

[9]Mark R. Leary et al., "Boredom in Interpersonal Encounters: Antecedents and Social Implications," *Journal of Personality and Social Psychology* 51, no. 5 (1986): 968-75.

[10]Orrin Edgar Klapp, *Overload and Boredom: Essays on the Quality of Life in the Information Society* (New York: Greenwood, 1986), p. 20.

[11]Patricia Meyer Spacks, *Boredom: The Literary History of a State of Mind* (Chicago: University of Chicago Press, 1995), p. 13.

[12]Ibid., p. 260.

[13]Blaise Pascal, *Mind on Fire: A Faith for the Skeptical and Indifferent*, ed. James M. Houston (Minneapolis: Bethany House, 1997), p. 61.

[14]Ibid., p. 100.

[15]Jacques Bossuet, *From M. A. Couturier, Se Garder Libre* (Paris: Editions du Cerf, 1962), p. 70.

[16]Seán Desmond Healy, *Boredom, Self and Culture* (Toronto: Associated University Presses, 1984), p. 30.

[17]Randle Cotgrave, *A Dictionarie of the French and English Tongues* (London, 1611), quoted in

ibid., p. 19.

[18]William Shakespeare, *King Henry IV, Part 2*, 4.5.93.

[19]Spacks, *Boredom*, chap. 2.

[20]Logan Pearsall Smith, *The English Language*, 3rd ed. (London: Oxford University Press, 1966), p. 131.

[21]Kuhn, *Demon of Noontide*, pp. 331, 375.

[22]Klapp, *Overload and Boredom*, pp. 11-12.

Chapter 2: Basics of Boredom

[1]Woodburn Heron, "The Pathology of Boredom," *Scientific American* 196 (January 1957): 54-56.

[2]Mihaly Csikszentmihalyi, *Flow: The Psychology of Optimal Experience* (New York: Harper Perennial, 1991), p. 91.

[3]Ibid., p. 91.

[4] Heron, "Pathology of Boredom," p. 52.

[5]Peter Conrad, "It's Boring: Notes on the Meanings of Boredom in Everyday Life," in *Qualitative Sociology as Everyday Life*, ed. Barry Glassner and Rosanna Hertz (Thousand Oaks, Calif.: Sage, 1999), p. 128.

[6]Mary B. Harris, "Correlates and Characteristics of Boredom Proneness and Boredom," *Journal of Applied Social Psychology* 30, no. 3 (2000): 586.

[7]Robert Kaplan et al., *Job Demands and Worker Health* (Washington, D.C.: U.S. Government Printing Office, 1975), quoted in Orrin Edgar Klapp, *Overload and Boredom: Essays on the Quality of Life in the Information Society* (New York: Greenwood, 1986), p. 14.

[8]S. Wyatt and J. A. Fraser assisted by F. G. L. Stock, "The Effects of Monotony in Work," *Industrial Health Research Board, Report No. 56*, p. 42, quoted in Elton Mayo, *The Human Problems of an Industrial Civilization*, 2nd ed. (Boston: Division of Research Graduate School of Business Administration, Harvard University, 1946), p. 32.

[9]J. M. Barbalet, "Boredom and Social Meaning," *British Journal of Sociology* 50 (December 1999): 64.

[10]Klapp, *Overload and Boredom*, p. 14.

[11]Michael J. Smith, Frank T. Conway and Ben-Tzion Karsh, "Occupational Stress in Human Computer Interaction," *Industrial Health* 37 (April 1999): 157-73.

[12]See Michael L. Raposa, *Boredom and the Religious Imagination* (Charlottesville: University Press of Virginia, 1999), pp. 105-35, on ritual and redundancy.

[13]Elaine Scarry, *On Beauty and Being Just* (Princeton, N.J.: Princeton University Press, 1999), p. 3.

[14]Conrad, "It's Boring," p. 130.

[15]Cynthia D. Fisher, "Boredom at Work: A Neglected Concept," *Human Relations* 46, no. 3 (1993): 395-417.

[16]Linda L. Caldwell et al., "Why Are You Bored? An Examination of Psychological and Social Control Causes of Boredom Among Adolescents," *Journal of Leisure Research* 31, no. 2 (1999): 103-21.

[17]George Eliot, *The Mill on the Floss* (New York: Oxford University Press, 1996), p. 291.

[18]Samuel Beckett, *Waiting for Godot: Tragicomedy in 2 Acts* (New York: Grove, 1982).

[19]Jerome Neu, "Boring from Within: Endogenous Versus Reactive Boredom," in *Emotions in Psychopathology*, ed. William F. Flack Jr. and James D. Laird (New York: Oxford University Press, 1998), p. 167.

Chapter 3: Two Types of Boredom

[1]See J. M. Barbalet, "Boredom and Social Meaning," *British Journal of Sociology* 50 (December 1999): 631-46; and Martin Waugh, "Boredom in Psychoanalytic Perspective," *Social Research* 42 (1975): 541.

[2]Joseph Brodsky, "Listening to Boredom," *Harper's*, March 1995, p. 11.

[3]Jan Burte and Daniel L. Araoz, "Paralysis of the Soul: When Life Becomes Boredom," in *Psychotherapy and the Bored Patient*, ed. E. Mark Stern (New York: Haworth, 1988), p. 157.

[4]Martha Hyneman, "Sloth," *Parabola*, winter 1985, pp. 16-18.

[5]Seán Desmond Healy, *Boredom, Self and Culture* (Toronto: Associated University Presses, 1984), p. 48.

[6]Barbalet, "Boredom and Social Meaning," p. 634.

[7]Patricia Meyer Spacks, *Boredom: The Literary History of a State of Mind* (Chicago: University of Chicago Press, 1995).

[8]Charles Dickens, *Bleak House* (1853; reprint, New York: Penguin, 1996), p. 449.

[9]George Eliot, *Daniel Deronda* (1876; reprint, New York: Penguin, 1995), p. 135.

[10]Fyodor Dostoevsky, *The Possessed* (New York: Modern Library, 1963), pp. 704-5, 711.

[11]Evelyn Waugh, *Vile Bodies* (Boston: Little, Brown & Company, 1930), pp. 170-71.

[12]Saul Bellow, *Humboldt's Gift* (New York: Avon, 1976).

[13]Spacks, *Boredom*, p. 265.

[14]Gregory Wolfe, "A Stranger and a Pilgrim," *Catholic World Report*, November 1991, p. 64, quoted in Steven Garber, *The Fabric of Faithfulness* (Downers Grove, Ill.: InterVarsity Press, 1996), p. 102.

[15]Linda L. Caldwell et al., "Why Are You Bored? An Examination of Psychological and Social Control Causes of Boredom Among Adolescents," *Journal of Leisure Research* 31, no. 2 (1999): 119.

Chapter 4: Entertained to Excess

[1]Robert Lee, *Religion and Leisure in America* (Nashville: Abingdon, 1964), p. 37.

[2]Mary Pipher, *The Shelter of Each Other: Rebuilding Our Families* (New York: Ballantine, 1996), pp. 39-40.

[3]Simon Shaw et al., *Frontier House* (New York: Atria Books, 2002), p. 216.

[4]Pipher, *Shelter*, p. 84.

[5]TV Turnoff Network facts <www.turnoff.com>.

[6]John P. Robinson and Geoffrey Godbey, *Time for Life: The Surprising Ways Americans Use Their Time*, 2nd ed. (University Park: Pennsylvania State University Press, 1999), pp. 124-26.

[7]Roger Scruton, *An Intelligent Person's Guide to Modern Culture* (London: Duckworth, 1998), p. 96.

[8]Wendell Berry, *What Are People For?* (San Francisco: North Point, 1990), pp. 158-59.

[9]Bernard Shaw, quoted in Robert Lee, *Religion and Leisure*, p. 25.

[10]Lee, *Religion and Leisure*, p. 23.

[11]Orrin Edgar Klapp, *Overload and Boredom: Essays on the Quality of Life in the Information Society* (New York: Greenwood, 1986), p. 40.

[12]Georg Simmel, *The Sociology of Georg Simmel*, ed. Kurt H. Wolff (New York: Free Press, 1950), p. 414.

[13]Patricia Meyer Spacks, *Boredom: The Literary History of a State of Mind* (Chicago: University of Chicago Press, 1995), p. 261..

[14]See <www.boringinstitute.com>, <www.dullmen.com> and <www.planetboredom.com>.

[15]William Wordsworth, "Preface to Lyrical Ballads, 1800," in *Selected Poems and Sonnets* (London: Holt, Rinehart & Winston, 1954), p. 7.

[16]Neal Gabler, *Life, the Movie: How Entertainment Conquered Reality* (New York: Alfred A. Knopf, 1999).

[17]Bill Watterson, *It's a Magical World: A Calvin and Hobbes Collection* (Kansas City, Mo.: Andrews & McMeel, 1996), p. 74.

[18]Lev Grossman, "Play Nation," *On Monthly: Supplement to Time Magazine*, June 2001, p. 26.

[19]"Letters," *Time*, June 17, 2002.

[20]Ibid., p. 35.

[21]Patrick DeGayardon, quoted in Joe Sector Sport Watches, "Sector No Limits" *Outside*, December 1997, p. 69.

[22]Ray Miller, quoted in Susan Enfield, "To the Pole . . . the One-Brick-Short-of-a-Load Way," *Outside*, December 1997, p. 30.

[23]John Middendorf, quoted in Craig Vetter, "Off Belay, Deano!" *Outside*, September 1995, pp. 104-5.

[24]Marvin Zuckerman, *Sensation Seeking: Beyond the Optimal Level of Arousal* (Hillsdale, N.J.: Lawrence Erlbaum Associates, 1979).

[25]Derek Lundy, *Godforsaken Sea: Racing the World's Most Dangerous Waters* (Chapel Hill, N.C.: Algonquin Books of Chapel Hill, 1998), p. 192.

[26]Karl Greenfield, "Life on the Edge," *Time*, September 6, 1999, p. 30.

[27]Glenn Zorpette, "Extreme Sports, Sensation Seeking and the Brain," *Scientific American Quarterly* 10 (1999): 56-57.

[28]Lundy, *Godforsaken Sea*, p. 32.

[29]Ibid., p. 6.

[30]Ibid., p. 15.

[31]Ibid., p. 184.

[32]Michael Gordon, "Surviving the Real World: Voyeur-Vision and the Quest for Reality," *Perspectives*, summer 2002, p. 6.

[33]See ibid., pp. 1-7.

[34]See Jock McGregor, "Surviving Reality TV," a L'Abri lecture in Rochester, Minnesota, on October 6, 2000.

[35]Robert MacNeil, "Is Television Shortening Our Attention Span?" *New York University Education Quarterly* 14 (1983): 2, quoted in Neil Postman, *Amusing Ourselves to Death: Public Discourse in the Age of Show Business* (New York: Penguin, 1985), p. 105.

[36]Gene Veith, "Boredom and the Law of Diminishing Returns," *AFA Journal*, January 1998, p. 20.

[37]Henry Fairlie, *The Seven Deadly Sins Today* (Washington, D.C.: New Republic Books, 1978), p. 125.

[38]T. S. Eliot, "East Coker," in *T. S. Eliot: The Complete Poems and Plays, 1909-1950* (New York: Harcourt Brace & Co., 1980), p. 126.

[39]T. S. Eliot, "Burnt Norton," in ibid., p. 120.

Chapter 5: Advertised to Apathy

[1]Richard Stivers, *The Culture of Cynicism: American Morality in Decline* (Cambridge, Mass.: Blackwell, 1994), p. 50.

[2]Ibid., pp. 50-52.

[3]Daniel I. Boorstin, *The Americans: The Democratic Experience* (New York: Random House, 1973), p. 129.

[4]Lendol Calder, "What Are Things For? An Essay on Living Faithfully as Christians in a Consumer Culture," *Critique*, no. 8 (Rochester, Minn.: Ransom Fellowship, 1990), pp. 1-11.

[5]Patricia Meyer Spacks, *Boredom: The Literary History of a State of Mind* (Chicago: University of Chicago Press, 1995), p. 249.

[6]Haskell E. Bernstein, "Boredom and the Ready-Made Life," *Social Research* 42, no. 3 (1975): 521.

[7]Spacks, *Boredom*, p. 249.

[8]Boorstin, *Americans*, p. 137.

[9]Stivers, *Culture of Cynicism*, p. 59, with a quote from Roland Marchand, *Advertising the American Dream* (Berkeley: University of California Press, 1985), p. 234.

[10]Joseph Pieper, *Four Cardinal Virtues* (Notre Dame, Ind.: Notre Dame University Press, 1966), p. 200.

[11]Bill Watterson, *It's a Magical World: A Calvin and Hobbes Collection* (Kansas City, Mo.: Andrews & McMeel, 1996), p. 40.

[12]C. S. Lewis, *The Last Battle* (New York: Collier, 1970), p. 148.

[13]Mary Pipher, *The Shelter of Each Other: Rebuilding Our Families* (New York: Ballantine, 1996), p. 81. "Thirsty in the Rain" is the title of a song by Peter Rowan on *Walls of Time* (Sugar Hill, 1982).

[14]Pipher, *Shelter*, p.15.

[15]Daniel Goleman, *Working with Emotional Intelligence* (New York: Bantam, 1998), p. 80.

[16]David Denby, "Buried Alive: Our Children and the Avalanche of Crud," *New Yorker*, July 15, 1996, pp. 48; 51.

[17]Todd Gitlin, in an interview with James Fallows in "Signals of Saturation," *The Atlantic Online*, April 3, 2002 <www.theatlantic.com/unbound/fallows/jf2002-04-03>.

[18]Neil Postman, *Amusing Ourselves to Death: Public Discourse in the Age of Show Business* (New York: Penguin, 1985), pp. 155; vii.

[19]Os Guinness, *The Call* (Nashville: Word, 1998), p. 149.

Chapter 6: Why Some People Are More Likely to Get Bored

[1]Peter Conrad, "It's Boring: Notes on the Meanings of Boredom in Everyday Life," chap. 13

of *Qualitative Sociology as Everyday Life*, ed. Barry Glassner and Rosanna Hertz (Thousand Oaks, Calif.: Sage, 1999), p. 126.

[2]William L. Mikulas and Stephen J. Vodanovich, "The Essence of Boredom," *Psychological Record* 43, no. 1 (1993): 3.

[3]Norman D. Sundberg et al., "Boredom in Young Adults: Gender and Cultural Comparisons," *Journal of Cross-Cultural Psychology* 22 (June 1991): 210.

[4]Timothy K. DeChenne and Andrea J. Moody, "Boredom: Theory and Therapy," in *Psychotherapy and the Bored Patient*, ed. E. Mark Stern (New York: Haworth, 1988), p. 19.

[5]Colin Cooper and Richard Taylor, "Personality and Performance on a Frustrating Cognitive Task," *Perceptual and Motor Skills* 88 (June 1999): 1384.

[6]Kathryn Greene et al., "Targeting Adolescent Risk-Taking Behaviors: The Contributions of Egocentrism and Sensation-Seeking," *Journal of Adolescence* 23 (August 2000): 445-46.

[7]Stephen J. Vodanovich and Deborah E. Rupp, "Are Procrastinators Prone to Boredom?" *Social Behavior and Personality* 27, no. 1 (1999): 11-16.

[8]J. Sommers and Stephen J. Vodanovich, "Boredom Proneness: Its Relationship to Psychological and Physical Health Symptoms," *Journal of Clinical Psychology* 56 (January 2000): 152-55.

[9]Used with permission from Richard F. Farmer and Norman D. Sundberg, "Boredom Proneness: The Development and Correlates of a New Scale," *Journal of Personality Assessment* 50, no. 1 (1986): 10, 15. Richard Farmer wrote (in personal communication), and Norman Sundberg agreed:

> We have not done normative studies of the Boredom Proneness Scale, and to my knowledge others haven't administered it to a sample of the general population. It has been used for research purposes. However, one can make rough comparisons with the college student population on which most of the research has been done. For instance with both the U.S. and Australian samples the Mean on the 28-item scale is between 10 and 11 (roughly 10.5) and the Standard Deviation is roughly 5.

(See Sundberg et al., "Boredom in Young Adults.") So the middle two-thirds would score between 5.5 and 15.5; and approximately speaking, those who score below 5 are very low on the Boredom Proneness Scale (which means they are not easily bored), and those who score above 15 are very high on the scale.

[10]Stephen J. Vodanovich and Steven J. Kass, "A Factor Analytical Study of the Boredom Proneness Scale," *Journal of Personality Assessment* 55, nos. 1 and 2 (1990): 115-23.

[11]Marvin Zuckerman, *Sensation Seeking: Beyond the Optimal Level of Arousal* (Hillsdale, N.J.: Lawrence Erlbaum Associates, 1979), p. 11.

[12]John D. Watt and Stephen J. Vodanovich, "Boredom Proneness and Psychosocial Development," *Journal of Psychology* 133, no. 3 (1999): 303-14.

[13]Zuckerman, *Sensation Seeking*, p. 10.

[14]Richard Woodward, "Cormac McCarthy's Venomous Fiction," *New York Times*, April 19, 1992, Sunday late edition, book review section.

[15]Peter A. Hancock and Paula A. Desmond, eds., *Stress, Workload and Fatigue* (Mahwah, N.J.: Lawrence Erlbaum Associates, 2001), pp. 271-72.

[16]Farmer and Sundberg, "Boredom Proneness," p. 15; Stephen J. Vodanovich, Kathryn M. Verner and Thomas V. Gilbride, "Boredom Proneness: Its Relationship to Positive and Negative

Affect," *Psychological Reports* 69 (1991): 1139-46.

[17]John D. Watt and Stephen J. Vodanovich, "Relationship Between Boredom Proneness and Impulsivity," *Psychological Reports* 70, no. 3 (1992): 688-90; Steven J. Kass and Stephen J. Vodanovich, "Boredom Proneness: Its Relationship to Type A Behavior Pattern and Sensation Seeking," *Psychology, a Journal of Human Behavior* 27, no. 3 (1990): 7-16.

[18]Alexander Tolor, "Boredom as Related to Alienation, Assertiveness, Internal-External Expectancy and Sleep Patterns," *Journal of Clinical Psychology* 45, no. 2 (1989): 260-65; Vodanovich, Verner and Gilbride, "Boredom Proneness."

[19]Farmer and Sundberg, "Boredom Proneness," pp. 4-17.

[20]Vodanovich, Verner and Gilbride, "Boredom Proneness"; Tolor, "Boredom."

[21]Watt and Vodanovich, "Relationship Between Boredom Proneness."

[22]Robert R. Provine, "Yawning as a Stereotyped Action Pattern and Releasing Stimulus," *Ethology* 72, no. 2 (1986): 109-22.

[23]Monica Greco, Ronald Baenninger and John Govern, "On the Context of Yawning: When, Where and Why?" *Psychological Record* 43 (spring 1993): 178-84.

[24]Ronald Baenninger, "Some Comparative Aspects of Yawning in *Belta spendens, Homo sapiens, Panthero leo* and *Papio sphinx,*" *Journal of Comparative Psychology* 101, no. 4 (1987): 349-54.

[25]Robert R. Provine and Heidi B. Hamernick, "Yawning: Effects of Stimulus Interest," *Bulletin of Psychonomic Society* 24, no. 6 (1986): 437-38.

[26]Ronald Baenninger, "On Yawning and Its Functions," *Psychonomic Bulletin and Review* 4, no. 2 (1997): 200.

[27]Ibid., p. 201.

[28]The artificial or self-induced yawn, most often seen when the cabin pressure is changing during the ascent or descent of a flight, is to relieve pressure on the eardrum by opening the eustachian tube between the middle and outer ear.

Chapter 7: Negated to Numbness

[1]Dan B. Allender, *The Wounded Heart*, rev. ed. (Colorado Springs: NavPress, 1995), and *The Healing Path: How the Hurts in Your Life Can Lead You to a More Abundant Life* (Colorado Springs: Waterbrook, 1999).

[2]Ralph R. Greenson, "On Boredom," *American Psychoanalytical Association Journal* 1, no. 1 (1953): 19-20.

[3]Jan Burte and Daniel L. Araoz, "Paralysis of the Soul: When Life Becomes Boredom," in *Psychotherapy and the Bored Patient*, ed. E. Mark Stern (New York: Haworth, 1988), p. 161.

[4]Douglas L. Gerardi and Samuel M. Natale, "The Bored and Boring Patient," in *Psychotherapy and the Bored Patient*, ed. E. Mark Stern (New York: Haworth, 1988), p. 32.

[5]Bruno Bettleheim, quoted in Johanna Tabin, "Some Lively Thoughts on Boredom," in *Psychotherapy and the Bored Patient*, ed. E. Mark Stern (New York: Haworth, 1988), p. 147.

[6]Albert Camus, *The Stranger*, trans. by Stuart Gilbert (New York: Random House, 1946), quoted in Seán Desmond Healy, *Boredom, Self and Culture* (Toronto: Associated University Presses, 1984), p. 49.

[7]Greenson, "On Boredom," pp. 19-20.

[8]Haskell E. Bernstein, "Boredom and the Ready-Made Life," *Social Research* 42, no. 2 (1975): 525-26.

[9]John T. Maltsberger, "Case Consultation, Mansur Zaskar: A Man Almost Bored to Death," *Suicide and Life-Threatening Behavior* 30, no. 1 (2000): 74.

[10]Herbert Hendin, "Growing Up Dead: Student Suicide," *American Journal of Psychotherapy* 29, no. 3 (1975): 328, 337, quoted in John T. Maltsberger, "Case Consultation, Mansur Zaskar: A Man Almost Bored to Death," *Suicide and Life-Threatening Behavior* 30, no. 1 (2000): 89.

[11]Otto Fenichel, "On the Psychology of Boredom," in *The Collected Papers of Otto Fenichel*, 1st ser., ed. Hanna Fenichel and David Rapaport (New York: W. W. Norton, 1934), p. 301.

[12]L. M. Andrews, *To Thine Own Self Be True* (New York: Doubleday, 1989).

[13]Peter McWilliams and John-Roger, *You Can't Afford the Luxury of a Negative Thought* (Los Angeles: Prelude, 1989), p. 375.

[14]Richard Bargdill, *Being Bored with One's Life: An Empirical Phenomenological Study* (Ann Arbor: University of Michigan Dissertation Services, 1999).

[15]Henri Nouwen, *Out of Solitude: Three Meditations on the Christian Life* (Notre Dame, Ind.: Ave Maria, 1974), p. 56.

[16]Burte and Araoz, "Paralysis of the Soul," p. 164.

Chapter 8: A Trip Back in Time

[1]Michael L. Raposa, *Boredom and the Religious Imagination* (Charlottesville, Va.: University Press of Virginia, 1999), pp. 20-21.

[2]The word has several spellings: *acedia, accidie, accidia, accydye* and *acedy*.

[3]Raposa, *Boredom*, pp. 12, 177 n. 2.

[4]Ibid., pp. 12, 13, 20, 17.

[5]Dante Alighieri, *Inferno*, canto 18, trans. John Sinclair (New York: Oxford University Press, 1961), p. 237; Raposa, *Boredom*, p. 26.

[6]*Webster's Third New International Dictionary* (Springfield, Mass.: Merriam-Webster, 1993).

[7]Geoffrey Chaucer, *The Canterbury Tales* (London: Penguin, 1951), p. 506.

[8]William F. May, *A Catalogue of Sins: A Contemporary Examination of Christian Conscience* (New York: Holt, Rinehart & Winston, 1967), pp. 195-96.

[9]B. B. Warfield, *The Religious Life of Theological Students* (Nutley, N.J.: Presbyterian & Reformed, 1952), p. 7.

[10]A dramatic account is given by the fourth-century physician John Cassian in his "Of the Spirit of Accidie" 10.1-10.2.

[11]Seán Desmond Healy, *Boredom, Self and Culture* (Toronto: Associated University Presses, 1984), p. 17.

[12]Raposa, *Boredom*, p. 24.

[13]Siegfried Wenzel, *The Sin of Sloth: Acedia in Medieval Thought and Literature* (Chapel Hill: University of North Carolina Press, 1967), p. 31.

[14]Stanley W. Jackson, "Acedia the Sin and Its Relationship to Sorrow and Melancholia in Medieval Times," *Bulletin of the History of Medicine* 55, no. 2 (1981): 179-80.

[15]Raposa, *Boredom*, p. 27.

[16]David of Augsburg *Formula Novitiorum* 51 (*Maximia Bibliotheca Verterum Patrum et Antiquorum Scriptorum Ecclesiasticorum*, ed. Marerin de la Bigne [Lyon, 1677; Genoa 1707], 13:438).

[17]Raposa, *Boredom*, pp. 28-31.

[18]Healy, *Boredom, Self and Culture*, p. 19, italics his.

[19]Robertson Davies, *One-Half of Robertson Davies* (New York: Viking, 1977), p. 65.

[20]Os Guinness, *The Call* (Nashville: Word, 1998), p. 147.

[21]T. H. Wright, *Deadly Sins and Living Virtues* (Edinburgh: T & T Clark, 1934), p. 74.

[22]Patricia Meyer Spacks, *Boredom: The Literary History of a State of Mind* (Chicago: University of Chicago Press, 1995), p. 51.

[23]William Cowper, "Letter to Lady Hesketh, October 13, 1798," in *Letters of William Cowper* (London: Macmillan, 1914), p. 314.

[24]Elizabeth Cosgrave et al., "Depression in Young People: A Growing Challenge for Primary Care," *Australian Family Physician* 29 (February 2000): 123-27.

[25]Andrew Solomon, "Personal History: Anatomy of Melancholy," *New Yorker*, January 12, 1998, p. 46.

[26]J. M. Barbalet, "Boredom and Social Meaning," *British Journal of Sociology* 50 (December 1999): 635.

[27]William Shakespeare, *Hamlet*, 2.2.303-5.

Chapter 9: From Sin to Self-Fulfillment

[1]James Fordyce, quoted in Patricia Meyer Spacks, *Boredom: The Literary History of a State of Mind* (Chicago: University of Chicago Press, 1995), p. 65.

[2]Samuel Butler, "Memoir of the Late John Pickard Owen," in *The Works of Samuel Butler*, ed. Henry Festing Jones and A. T. Bartholomew (New York: AMS, 1968), 3:42.

[3]John Berryman, Dream Song #14, from *The Dream Songs* (New York: Farrar, Straus and Giroux, 1969).

[4]The inner resource of imagination is a bit more complicated because it can help or hinder. It might relieve boredom by creating an inner fantasy world to compensate for the poverty of the outer world; but it might also contribute to boredom because it is imagination that, by contrast, makes one aware of other possibilities and highlights the tedium of the present situation.

[5]*The Mirror* no. 106 (Edinburgh, 1780), quoted in Spacks, *Boredom*, p. 20. This phrase leaves the reader with an ambivalent feeling about the responsibility of the "victim." Disease usually implies something that comes on us through no fault of our own.

[6]Emily Post, *Etiquette: The Blue Book of Social Usage* (New York: Funk & Wagnalls, 1945), p. 46.

[7]American Humanist Association, Humanist Manifesto II (1973) <www.humanist.net/documents/manifesto2.html>.

[8]Spacks, *Boredom*, pp. 259-60.

[9]Carl Rogers, *On Becoming a Person: A Therapist's View of Psychotherapy* (Boston: Houghton Mifflin, 1961), pp. 23-24, italics his.

[10]Orrin Edgar Klapp, *Overload and Boredom: Essays on the Quality of Life in the Information Society* (New York: Greenwood, 1986), p. 27.

[11]Émile Durkheim, *Suicide: A Study in Sociology* (1987; reprint, New York: Free Press, 1979), p. 253.

[12]Klapp, *Overload and Boredom*, p. 256.

Chapter 10: Haunted by Hopelessness

[1]*The Matrix*, dir. Larry and Andy Wachowski (Warner Bros., 1999). For a discussion of *The Matrix*, see Denis Haack, "There's Something Wrong with the World: Virtual Reality Versus Reality," *Critique*, no. 7 (Rochester, Minn.: Ransom Fellowship, 1999), pp. 5-7.

[2]*American Beauty*, dir. Sam Mendes (DreamWorks, 2000).

[3]*Run Lola Run*, written and directed by Tom Tykwer (Sony Picture Classics, 1998). For discussion of this movie, see Denis Haack, "A Race for Life in a Fragmented World," *Critique*, no. 8 (Rochester, Minn.: Ransom Fellowship, 1999), pp. 6-7.

[4]Jacques Derrida, *Positions*, trans. and ed. Alan Bass (London: Athlene, 1987).

[5]Michael Williams, "Speaking the Gospel in Postmodernist Ears," *Presbyterion* 26 (2000): 16.

[6]*Reality Bites*, dir. Ben Stiller (Universal City Studios, 1994), quoted in Steven Garber, *The Fabric of Faithfulness* (Downers Grove, Ill.: InterVarsity Press, 1996), p. 143.

[7]James Kunen, "It Ain't Us Babe!" *Time*, September 1, 1997, pp. 66-67.

[8]Dorothy Sayers, quoted in Henry Fairlie, *The Seven Deadly Sins Today* (Washington, D.C.: New Republic Books, 1978), p. 114.

[9]Peter Kreeft, *Christianity for Modern Pagans: Pascal's Pensées Edited, Outlined and Explained* (San Francisco: Ignatius, 1993), p. 188.

[10]Friedrich Nietzsche, *The Antichrist*, trans. H. L. Mencken (1888; reprint, Torrance, Calif.: Noontide, 1980), p. 137.

[11]Patricia Meyer Spacks, *Boredom: The Literary History of a State of Mind* (Chicago: University of Chicago Press, 1995), p. 114.

[12]Ibid., p. 21. Spacks is quoting William F. Lynch, *Images of Faith: An Exploration of the Ironic Imagination* (Notre Dame, Ind.: University of Notre Dame Press, 1974), p. 99.

[13]Seán Desmond Healy, *Boredom, Self and Culture* (Toronto: Associated University Presses, 1984), p. 87.

[14]Martin Heidegger, *An Introduction to Metaphysics* (Garden City, N.Y.: Doubleday/Anchor, 1961), pp. 1-2; Martin Heidegger, "What Is Metaphysics?" in *Existence and Being*, ed. W. Brock (Chicago: Henry Regnery, 1949), p. 364.

[15]Georges Bernanos, *The Diary of a Country Priest* (Garden City, N.Y.: Dell/Delta, 1956), pp. 295-96, quoted in Healy, *Boredom*, p. 34.

[16]Pierre Teilhard de Chardin, *The Future of Man* (New York: Harper & Row, 1969), pp. 150-51.

[17]Karl Jaspers, *Man in the Modern Age* (London: Routledge & Kegan Paul, 1959), p. 25.

[18]Friedrich Nietzsche, *The Will to Power*, ed. Walter Kaufman (New York: Vintage, 1968), pp. 20, 331, italics his.

[19]W. B. Yeats, "The Second Coming," in *The Collected Poems of W. B. Yeats*, ed. Richard J. Finneran, 2nd ed. (New York: Scribner Paperback Poetry, 1996), p. 187.

[20]Heidegger, "What Is Metaphysics?" p. 366.

[21]Healy, *Boredom, Self and Culture*, p. 53.

[22]Friedrich Nietzsche, *The Gay Science*, trans. Walter Kaufmann (New York: Vintage, 1974), p. 182.

[23]Healy, *Boredom, Self and Culture*, pp. 91, 90.

[24]Nietzsche, *Gay Science*, p. 280.

[25]Jean Paul Sartre, *Existentialism and Humanism* (London: Eyre Methuen, 1982), p. 54.

[26]Mihaly Csikszentmihalyi, *Flow: The Psychology of Optimal Experience* (New York: Harper Perennial, 1991), p. 215.

[27]Ibid., p. 225, 227.

[28]Ibid., p. 240.

[29]Victor Frankl, *Man's Search for Meaning* (New York: Washington Square Press, 1969).

[30]John McLaren, "Life on the Links Is Not a Young Man's Game," *The Sunday Times* (London), November 18, 2001, News Review sec., p. 7.

[31]Augustine *The Confessions* 1.1.

[32]Blaise Pascal, *Mind on Fire: A Faith for the Skeptical and Indifferent*, ed. James M. Houston (Minneapolis: Bethany House, 1997), p. 97.

[33]Jacques Ellul, quoted in Mark Fackler, "Teens and Their Raggedy Questions," *Discernment* 5 (1998): 1.

[34]Walker Percy, *Lost in the Cosmos: The Last Self-Help Book* (New York: Noonday, 1992), pp. 70-71.

[35]Andrew Fellows, "The Self at the Dawn of a New Millennium," *Lev International: The International Newsletter of L'Abri Fellowship*, summer 2000, p. 6.

[36]Healy, *Boredom, Self and Culture*, p. 113.

[37]Ibid., p. 110.

[38]Blaise Pascal, *Pensées*, trans. A. J. Krailsheimer (Baltimore: Penguin, 1966), p. 75.

[39]William Shakespeare, *As You Like It*, 2.1.16-17.

[40]Northrop Frye, *T. S. Eliot* (New York: Grove, 1963).

[41]A. E. Carter, *Charles Baudelaire* (Boston: Twayne, 1977), p. 100.

Chapter 11: The Bitter Fruits of Boredom

[1]Alex Blaszczynski, Neil McConaghy and Anna Frankova, "Boredom Proneness in Pathological Gambling," *Psychological Reports* 67 (August 1990): 127-42; Lloyd D. Johnston and Patrick M. O'Malley, "Why Do the Nation's Students Use Drugs and Alcohol? Self-Reported Reasons from Nine National Surveys," *Journal of Drug Issues* 16 (winter 1986): 29-66; Richard M. Ganley, "Emotion and Eating in Obesity: A Review of Literature," *International Journal of Eating Disorders* 8, no. 3 (1989): 343-61.

[2]Marcella I. Stickney and Raymond G. Miltenberger, "Evaluating Direct and Indirect Measures for the Functional Assessment of Binge Eating," *International Journal of Eating Disorders* 26 (September 1999): 195-204.

[3]Georgette K. Maroldo, "Shyness, Boredom and Grade Point Average Among College Students," *Psychological Reports* 59 (October 1986): 395-98; W. P. Robinson, "Boredom at School," *British Journal of Educational and Psychology* 45, no. 2 (1975): 141-52.

[4]See James F. O'Hanlon, "Boredom: Practical Consequences and a Theory," *Acta Psychological* 49, no. 1 (1981): 53-82; Paul Branton, "A Field Study of Repetitive Manual Work in Relation to Accidents at the Work Place," *International Journal of Production Research* 8, no. 2 (1970): 93-107; Bertil Gardell, "Alienation and Mental Health in the Modern Industrial Environment," *Society, Stress and Disease*, ed. Lennart Levi (New York: Oxford University Press, 1971), 1:148-80; and Cynthia D. Fisher, "Boredom at Work: A Neglected Concept," *Human*

Relations 46, no. 3 (1993): 395-417.

[5]Søren Kierkegaard, "The Rotation Method," *Either/Or,* trans. David F. Swenson and Lillian Marvin Swenson (Princeton, N.J.: Princeton University Press, 1944), 1:234.

[6]Tibor Scitovsky, "The Wages of Boredom," *New Perspectives Quarterly* 17 (spring 2000): 45-46.

[7]Eric Hoffer, *The True Believer* (New York: Perennial Library, 1989), pp. 51-52.

[8]Dennis de Rougemont, *The Devil's Share* (New York: Pantheon, 1944), p. 153.

[9]C. S. Lewis, *The Screwtape Letters* (New York: Penguin, 1988), pp. 33, 34.

[10]Patricia Meyer Spacks, *Boredom: The Literary History of a State of Mind* (Chicago: University of Chicago Press, 1995), pp. 259-60.

[11]Cyril Connolly, *The Unquiet Grave: A Word Cycle by Palinurus,* rev. ed. (1944; reprint, New York: Persea, 1981), p. 31.

[12]Donald McCullough, "Anything but Boredom!" *Christianity Today,* August 19, 1991, p. 31.

[13]Rollo May, *Psychology and the Human Dilemma* (New York: Van Nostran, 1967), p. 42, quoted in Dick Keyes, *Beyond Identity* (Carlisle, U.K.: Paternoster, 1998), p. 32.

[14]These statistics were gathered in 2000.

[15]Frank Rich, "Naked Capitalists," *New York Times Magazine,* May 20, 2001, sec. 6, p. 51.

[16]Anna Grear, "Pornography: Inciting Sexual Hatred," *Today,* January 1991, p. 8.

[17]Philip Elmer-Dewitt, "On the Screen Near You: Cyberporn," *Time,* July 3, 1995, p. 42.

[18]William Anderson, quoted in Ron Powers, "The Apocalypse of Adolescence," *Atlantic Monthly,* March 2002, p. 68.

[19]Theo Padnos, quoted in Powers, "Apocalypse of Adolescence," pp. 68-69.

[20]Roy Baumeister and Keith W. Campbell, "The Intrinsic Appeal of Evil: Sadism, Sensational Thrills and Threatened Egotism," *Personality and Social Psychology Review* 3, no. 3 (1999): 215. See J. Katz, *Seduction of Crime: Moral and Sensual Attractions in Doing Evil* (New York: Basic Books, 1988).

[21]Kathryn Greene et al., "Targeting Adolescent Risk-Taking Behaviors: The Contribution of Egocentrism and Sensation Seeking," *Journal of Adolescence* 23 (August 2000): 439-61.

[22]Kim Witte and William A. Donohue, "Preventing Vehicle Crashes with Trains at Grade Crossings: The Risk Seeker Challenge," *Accident Analysis and Prevention* 32 (January 2000): 127-42.

[23]Baumeister and Campbell, "The Intrinsic Appeal of Evil," p. 216.

[24]Wyn Craig Wade, *The Fiery Cross: The Ku Klux Klan in America* (New York: Oxford University Press, 1987), p. 34.

Chapter 12: Counteracting Boredom

[1]Kathy Peel, "Boredom Busters for Kids," *Family Circle,* June 25, 1996, p. 41; Stan Berenstain, *The Berenstain Bears with Nothing to Do* (New York: Golden Books, 1993); Wendy Smolen and Lisa Chudnofsky, "Summer's Hottest Toys: Flying Saucers, Race Cars, Sand Drills, Water Games and More! These Are the Best Boredom Busters Under the Sun," *Parents,* June 1, 1999, p. 141.

[2]Patricia Meyer Spacks, *Boredom: The Literary History of a State of Mind* (Chicago: University of Chicago Press, 1995), p. 3.

[3]Friedrich Nietzsche, *The Gay Science,* trans. Walter Kaufmann (New York: Vintage, 1974), p. 108, quoted in Spacks, *Boredom,* p. 2.

[4]Anna Quindlen, "Doing Nothing Is Something," *Newsweek,* May 13, 2002, p. 76.

[5]Mary Pipher, *The Shelter of Each Other: Rebuilding Our Families* (New York: Ballantine, 1996), p. 90.

[6]Paul Persall, quoted in Richard Simon, "Don't Just Do Something, Sit There," *Family Therapy Networker* 23, no 1 (1999): 36.

[7]Jerome Neu, "Boring from Within: Endogenous Versus Reactive Boredom," in *Emotions in Psychopathology,* ed. William F. Flack Jr. and James D. Laird (New York: Oxford University Press, 1998), p. 168 n. 3.

[8]Thomas Dubay, *The Evidential Power of Beauty* (San Francisco: Ignatius, 1999), p. 72, with a quote from Lewis Thomas, "On Life in a Hell of a Place," *Discover,* October 1983, pp. 42, 321.

[9]Ron Taffel, "Discovering Our Children," *Family Therapy Networker* 23, no 5 (1999): 27.

[10]Tibor Scitovsky, "Boredom: An Overlooked Disease?" *Challenge* 42 (September-October 1999): 8, 13.

[11]Mary B. Harris, "Correlates and Characteristics of Boredom Proneness and Boredom," *Journal of Applied Social Psychology* 30, no. 3 (2000): 592.

[12]Geoffrey Chaucer, "The Parson's Sermon," in *The Canterbury Tales,* quoted in Henry Fairlie, *The Seven Deadly Sins Today* (Washington, D.C.: New Republic Books, 1978), p. 123.

[13]Spacks, *Boredom,* p. 140.

[14]Robert Jean Campbell, *The Psychiatric Dictionary* (New York: Oxford University Press, 1996), p. 102.

[15]Mihaly Csikszentmihalyi, "If We Are So Rich, Why Aren't We Happy?" *The American Psychologist* 54, no. 10 (1999): 826.

[16]Mihaly Csikszentmihalyi, *Flow: The Psychology of Optimal Experience* (New York: Harper Perennial, 1991), p. xi.

[17]Ibid., p. 3.

[18]Ibid., p. 45.

[19]Ibid., p. 3.

[20]Ibid., p. 53.

[21]Ibid., p. 56.

[22]Ibid., p. 158-59.

[23]Ibid., pp. 162, 163

[24]Fairlie, *Seven Deadly Sins,* p. 126.

[25]Pipher, *Shelter,* p. 94.

[26]Stephen J. Vodanovich and John D. Watt, "The Relationship Between Time Structure and Boredom Proneness," *Journal of Social Psychology* 139, no. 2 (1999): 143-52.

[27]Dubay, *Evidential Power,* pp. 73-74.

Chapter 13: Not So Easy, Not So Fast

[1]Josef Pieper, *Leisure: The Basis of Culture* (1948; reprint, South Bend, Ind.: St. Augustine's Press, 1998).

[2]Os Guinness, *The Call* (Nashville: Word, 1998), pp. 146-47.

[3]Sebastian de Grazia, *Of Time, Work and Leisure* (Garden City, N.Y.: Anchor Books, 1964), p. 325, quoted in Dennis Haack, "Boredom: Adam & Eve Rested, but Were They Ever Bored?"

Critique 1 (2000): 5.

[4]See David Myers, "Wealth, Well-Being, and the New American Dream" <www .newdream.org/discuss/myers.html>; see also his *The American Paradox: Spiritual Hunger in an Age of Plenty* (New Haven, Conn.: Yale University Press, 2000); and *The Pursuit of Happiness* (New York: Morrow, 1992).

[5]Mihaly Csikszentmihalyi, "If We Are So Rich, Why Aren't We Happy?" *American Psychologist* 54, no. 10 (1999): 823.

[6]Stephen Linder, *The Harried Leisure Class* (New York: Columbia University Press, 1970).

[7]Ibid. See also M. Benedikt, *Values* (Austin: University of Texas Press, 1999); Tibor Scitovsky, *The Joyless Economy* (New York: Random House, 1975).

[8]Jerome Neu, "Boring from Within: Endogenous Versus Reactive Boredom," in *Emotions in Psychopathology*, ed. William F. Flack Jr. and James D. Laird (New York: Oxford University Press, 1998), pp. 163-64.

[9]Ibid., p. 163.

[10]Ibid., p. 166.

[11]Ibid., p. 167.

[12]William F. May, *A Catalogue of Sins: A Contemporary Examination of Christian Conscience* (New York: Holt, Rinehart & Winston, 1967), pp. 196-97.

[13]John Calvin *Institutes of the Christian Religion* (Battles) 2.6.1.

[14]G. K. Chesterton, *Orthodoxy* (San Francisco: Ignatius, 1995), p. 66.

[15]*The Thin Red Line*, dir. Terrence Malick (Twentieth Century Fox, 1998).

[16]*Chariots of Fire*, written by Collin Welland, directed by Hugh Hudson (Enigma, 1981).

[17]Samuel Johnson, quoted in Haack, "Boredom," p. 5.

Chapter 14: Why Get Up in the Morning?

[1]J. R. R. Tolkien, *The Hobbit* (New York: Ballantine, 1983), p. 15.

[2]John Eldredge, *Wild at Heart* (Nashville: Thomas Nelson, 2000), chaps. 1-2.

[3]Dennis de Rougemont, *The Devil's Share* (New York: Pantheon, 1944), pp. 152-53.

[4]John Ortberg, *The Life You've Always Wanted* (Grand Rapids, Mich.: Zondervan, 1997), p. 64.

[5]Seán Desmond Healy, *Boredom, Self and Culture* (Toronto: Associated University Press, 1984), p. 48.

[6]Arthur Schopenhauer, *The World as Will and Idea* (London: Routledge & Kegan Paul, 1957), 1:215.

[7]C. S. Lewis, *The Weight of Glory* (San Francisco: HarperSanFrancisco, 2001), pp. 30-31.

[8]Os Guinness, *The Call* (Nashville: Word, 1998), p. 151.

Name Index

Subject Index